Creation Anatomy:

A Study Guide to the Miracles of the Body!

by

Felice Gerwitz and Jill Whitlock

Creation Anatomy: A Study Guide to the Miracles of the Body.
Media Angels® Inc.
Ft. Myers, FL 33912
© 1996, 1997, 2016, Felice Gerwitz and Jill Whitlock
© 2016, Felice Gerwitz
All rights reserved.

MediaAngels.com

Printed in the United States of America

ISBN# 1-931941-43-2

ISBN# 978-1-931941-43-3

All scripture quotations are taken from The New International Version, Grand Rapids, Zondervan Bible Publishers, 1983.

This book is dedicated to

our children, the miracles in our lives:

Neal, Christina, Nicholas, Anne, and Michael Gerwitz

Jacob, Jonathan, Jesse Whitlock

"The body is a unit, though it is made up of many parts; and though all its parts are many, they form one body. So it is with Christ. For we are all baptized by one Spirit into one body…" 1 Corinthians 12:12

Table of Contents

Introduction To Creation Anatomy

The human body is the most amazing handiwork in all of God's creation. The amazing flexibility of the structure that is totally self-contained and self-propelled is remarkable. To think that anything as complicated as the human body could have evolved by random chance processes requires more faith than our belief in Creation. As you study each fascinating system in the body, with its precisely designed functions, you will be amazed and will truly appreciate how you were created. Not only is each system special, but they are all interrelated and interdependent. Just as God stated, when He compared the Body of Christ to the human body, every function is unique but each is dependent on all the others.

"The body is a unit, though it is made up of many parts; and though all its parts are many, they form one body. So it is with Christ. For we were all baptized by one Spirit into one body - whether Jews or Greeks, slave or free - and we were all given the one Spirit to drink.

"Now the body is not made up of one part but of many. If the foot should say, 'Because I am not a hand, I do not belong to the body.' And if the ear should say, 'Because I am not an eye, I do not belong to the body,' it would not for that reason cease to be part of the body. If the whole body were an eye, where would the sense of hearing be? If the whole body were an ear, where would the sense of smell be? *But in fact God has arranged the parts in the body, every one of them, just as He wanted them to be.* If they were all one part, where would the body be? As it is, there are many parts, but one body.

"The eye cannot say to the hand, 'I don't need you!' And the head cannot say to the feet, 'I don't need you!' On the contrary, those parts of the body that seem to be weaker are indispensable, and the parts that we think are less honorable we treat with special honor. And the parts that are unpresentable are treated with special modesty, while our presentable parts need no special treatment. But God has combined the members of the body and has given greater honor to the parts that lacked it, so that there should be no division in the body, but that its parts should have equal concern for each other. If one part suffers, every part suffers with it; if one part is honored, every part rejoices with it.

"*Now you are the body of Christ, and each one of you is a part of it.*" (1 Corinthians 12:12-27) [*author's emphasis*]

God gives considerable importance to the body and to the Body of Christ. Christ gave His Body and His Blood for us . In this unit we will learn the importance of each body part and its significance. I hope you enjoy doing this unit as much as I enjoyed researching it!

Jill Whitlock

Editor's Note: Jill went to be with the Lord in 2007. She will forever be missed, but her work lives on and continues to touch lives. I pray you enjoy this unit.

Creation Anatomy:
A Study Guide to the Miracles of the Body

By
Felice Gerwitz and Jill Whitlock

Media Angels® Inc.
Fort Myers, Florida

How This Study Works

The *Creation Anatomy unit study* has and continues to be a popular curriculum choice for educators who wish to incorporate the study of anatomy into their science selections for their students. The study's first publication in 1996, written by Felice Gerwitz and the late Jill Whitlock, has been revised to encompass innovative teaching ideas within each grade division, as well as optional lesson plans for teachers, including a quick reference/teaching format ideas in regard to the implementation of the text's content.

The following section provides the reader with comments from both authors pertaining to the importance of studying anatomy from a creation viewpoint, a section describing what constitutes a unit study, how to prepare a unit study and various Q&A's often related to the topic of unit studies.

To allow for easier access, the unit study has been divided into three main sections: Section 1—Teaching Outline and Outline Content; Section 2—Grades K -3; Grades 4-8; Grades 9-12 and Section 3—Additional Resources.

In addition, each grade division contains a study outline, sample lesson plans, reading list, activity/experiment resource list, vocabulary/spelling list, vocabulary/spelling/grammar ideas, math reinforcement ideas, science activities/ experiments, geography/history ideas and art/music ideas.

As a supplement you may wish to purchase the companion book, *Creation Anatomy: Hands on Science and Activity Pack* available on Media Angels, Inc. While not necessary, this activity pack contains printables you will find helpful.

The prayer of the authors is the content of this unit study will not only help educators in their quest of teaching anatomy but also inspire them as well. Learning should be a fun experience for educator and student. When learning is fun, hands-on and messy, the experience is lasting. Try not to get bogged down and become a slave to a schedule—a recipe for disaster! Get ready to have a great time, and better yet, teach in a way that makes great memories that are cherished year after year after year.

> *I asked the whole frame of the world about my God; and he answered, I am not He, but He made me."*—-St. Augustine

Let's Do A Creation Anatomy Unit

The study of anatomy truly shows the awesomeness of our God! It is a study of the wonderful miracle God has created. *Anatomy* is the study of the *body's structure* while *physiology* is the study of *how the body works*. For this unit we will combine the meanings for the purpose of simplicity but will study both. We will study the *body's structure* and *how the body works*. We will also study the *blood; healing; digestive, nervous,* and *reproductive systems; DNA; the senses; the brain; language; races; and human history.* You will need to use discretion when teaching this unit, especially in the area of reproduction. As parents you know your children best and the *time* in which you plan to teach reproduction is up to you.

Science deals with the search for knowledge. In order for a scientific theory to be *valid*, it must be proved or disproved by testing or measuring. This is not possible with many of the theories or assumptions scientists have come up with to support claims about evolution. This book looks at science from a Creation viewpoint. No one was present when Almighty God created man; scientists can at best only theorize as to our origin. Therefore, I consider faith to be an issue whether you believe in Creation or evolution. (See *Creation Science: A Study Guide to Creation!*)

In this study of the human body you will be awed by the Creator's works. To believe that the complicated mechanisms of our bodies were created by an evolving process over millions of years is to miss the foundations that are self-evident in scientific study, especially in the area of DNA.

In researching Anatomy, you will find that various television shows, videos, books, articles, and computer programs almost exclusively deal with evolution. This study is meant to be a balance and to give you Creation Science's answers to evolution's claims so that your children can have a firm basis to dispute evolution.

In this unit we will explore the different contributions by *scientists* and a *history of anatomy.* In order to get the most from this unit study, it is important to have a firm, basic understanding of Creation Science, especially in the older grades, where an understanding of origins is desirable when comparing the two theories.

In this study, I have included the *ideas* I have found to be the most helpful. Many of the *games* and *activities* are original and have been played by children in science workshops I have given and at home with my own children. Some are old favorites revised a little to fit the occasion. In addition to the books listed as resources, I have included other resources, as you know information from Internet tend to be transient—so they are up to date as of this printing. There is a materials list and field trip guide. The pages containing information on the scientific method, you may copy to assist you with your experiments.

An important point in this science unit study is a correct execution of the *scientific method.* The *scientific method* is a procedure used to do an experiment in an organized fashion. *The point of the scientific method is to solve a problem or further investigate an observation*. The steps of the scientific method are as follows: *asking a question, researching, forming an educated guess as to what the conclusion will be, doing the experiment, observing the results, and stating a conclusion.* Ideally the conclusion should be the answer to the original question, but alas, things being what they are, this is not always the case! When learning a new scientific concept, make sure you have your children tell you in their own words what they have just learned. For example, let's say you are teaching them about the heart. You may want to do an experiment showing the heartbeat can be measured. To demonstrate your point, you will have your children jog in place for one minute (younger children) to five minutes (for the older ones), then measure their pulse. Be sure to ask questions such as, "How did you feel after you ran?" or "How do you know that your heart increased in speed?" They should be able to tell you, "We know our heart increased in speed because we can feel it beating faster." (Older children should be able to make a comparison between a faster beating heart and more oxygen being supplied to all of the body's systems through the blood.) This is a quick check to make sure they are following the concept and not getting sidetracked by the fun!

Science is always fun, but anatomy can be quite challenging! It is an especially humbling journey, one in which we should daily thank God for the miracle He has given us---our bodies!

Felice Gerwitz

How to Prepare a Unit Study

Understanding the composition and structural format of implementing a unit study into your curriculum is important. Without providing an exhaustive list, we have chosen to list some of the more popular Q&A's regarding unit studies in the hope you will find the information helpful as you prepare to teach Creation anatomy using this study guide. For additional information, we recommend *How to Create Your Own Unit Study* by Valerie Bendt.

What is a unit study?

A unit study is taking one topic, in this case Creation Anatomy, and interrelating all the other subjects into a unified teaching approach. In other words, while studying the topic of anatomy, the children will *read anatomy* science books and research materials, *write* assignments relating to what they've read, *spell* words they may have had difficulty reading or writing, *learn* vocabulary words dealing with anatomy, do *math problems* based on scientific principles, read and research *historical periods* relating to anatomy and time periods in which noteworthy evolutionists or Creation scientists lived, study *geographical locations* of scientific discoveries and Biblical events, create *art works* dealing with anatomy (such as drawing of the body) and for m*usic* play instruments using sounds produced by our vocal cords or other parts of the body (hands to clap rhythms, etc.). In other words, all the subjects will relate to the main topic. (The authors suggest you supplement grammar, phonics and math with other programs, where age appropriate.)

Why teach a unit study?

The unit study approach emphasizes that reading many books interrelated to a topic, rather than isolated textbooks, encourages discussion and research on the part of the children, therefore making learning more natural and retention of information much more successful. This is ideal for parents with children at different grade levels. It makes teaching much easier. The main area of interest can be taught in a group; then children can work on age-appropriate activities individually. It keeps the family together most of the time, rather than separating children to do their own individual work. It also encourages older siblings to assist younger ones and thereby learn by teaching.

How do I begin planning?

The best place to start is with a calendar, paper, pencil and the *Teaching Outline* in the study guide. The outline will help you become familiar with the topic. A unit study takes planning to be covered well. Write out a rough outline of the points you want to cover. You may use the outline points provided in each of the three grade levels, or you may utilize them as starters in creating your own outline. As you write your outline or points you want to cover, leave room for additions, i.e. you may run across a book or topic that you want to include. Decide how long you want your unit to take. What months are you considering? Is this time before a major holiday? If so, you may want to do a shorter unit. Is it the beginning of school, summer, or other longer period of time? If so, you may wish to do a more complicated unit or spend more time digging deeper into the topic you choose. Decide what subjects you want to incorporate and what days you will do each. For example you can spend every day reading, writing, doing grammar and math, but perhaps science experimentation and history will only be done three out of five days. You might prefer a Monday, Wednesday, Friday/ Tuesday, Thursday type of routine. Or, if you take Fridays off, your schedule might be Monday—Wednesday / Tuesday—Thursday. Remember, each family is unique and only you can decide which teaching/scheduling format is best suited for you and your students. *Feel free to use our suggested and detailed lesson plans with each grade level division.*

How do I begin using the Creation Study Guides?

It doesn't take much time to plan, especially with our study guides. We have done much of the planning and research for you with our detailed lesson plans. You don't need to use them but they are there for you. In addition, we have provided each grade division with additional subject related lists that will allow you to incorporate other subjects into the unit study as well.

The *Teaching Outline* is specifically to be read by the parent as preparation for teaching the topic. It will give you the necessary information and background necessary to teach the unit. We encourage you to read portions aloud to younger children and have older children read them alone or with you.

Again, planning is important. Have a calendar handy and map out the number of weeks you would like to spend on this unit. Approximately 6-8 weeks is a good time span for Creation science. (We feel this is an excellent preparation to counter secular materials where it is almost impossible to avoid the evolutionary viewpoint.)

How do unit studies differ from traditional teaching methods?

Traditionally subjects are taught in an isolated manner in textbooks or workbooks with fill-in-the-blank format. Very few, if any, of the subjects are interrelated, and all of the learning is done in an individual manner. Unit studies relate all academic subjects under one main idea and can easily work with one child or a group of children.

Does a unit study cover all of the topics I need to teach in every grade?

Yes and no! It depends on the grade level of your child and what your goals are for your home school. Many children know all they need to know for kindergarten by the time they are preschool aged. Thus, the kindergarten year is left free to implement unit studies on many different topics. Often, as the child progresses, because of all the reading research, projects and experimentation that he does, his learning will surpass what is generally considered normal for his grade level. Still, if you are concerned about standardized testing, the authors recommend you use these study guides as supplements to your core curriculum. However, in many cases, when homeschool students who have been taught with the unit study approach take a standardized test, they score in the 90+ percentile.

How long does it take to complete a unit study?

Unit studies can take several weeks or all year depending on how in-depth your coverage of a topic and the varying abilities of your children. In the younger grades you will most likely do an overview; in the middle grades you will do the unit building upon previous knowledge; and in the older grades you can do an in-depth study, delving deeper. For example we have used Creation Anatomy in our family as a unit study covering three months. We will use it again as a core subject for a high school science credit when the time comes. With units you are not bound to a structured one hour for each subject routine. The relationships between the topics are natural, and you will often find many subjects are covered without much effort. You will also be free to spend more time on a particularly interesting topic as you see your children's interest level rise in that area. These study guides are meant to be supplemental to your core curriculum, and you can tailor them to meet your family's needs.

Once you have an approximate time span, you will want to go through the age-appropriate outlines and lesson plans. If you have older and younger children, try to find a middle ground as a starting place. Look through the activities and suggested assignments. Check off the activities that interest you in each subject area. Decide which supplemental books you will need and plan on obtaining them. Interlibrary loans are able to obtain books from private as well as public libraries. We don't suggest you use every book we recommend. We usually list a greater number of books than necessary so that if you can't obtain one particular book, you may be able to find another.

I've decided what I want to teach; now how do I implement it all?!

Once you have chosen your materials and have your books, you can establish a calendar that reflects your instructional approach, i.e. strict methods or a more lenient approach. This depends on your family's needs and character. We have done both, and I have found that being more organized works for us. If you feel more secure having it all mapped out, please do so. You will know which days you are going to read and research, which days will be for spelling work, math and grammar, and which days you will be doing those experiments that are so important for hands-on learning! If you are an experienced homeschooler with an idea of what you want to accomplish and like to wing it, then go for it. If this approach doesn't work, you can always change it. The main thing to remember is not to become discouraged or feel overwhelmed.

One way to fit everything in is a day-to-day approach. You may want to do all the reading and research on day one, geography and history on day two, math, language arts (vocabulary, spelling and grammar) on day three, science experiments on day four, art and music on day five. Day five can also be used as the catch-up day, meaning you will finish any work not completed on the previous four days.

Decide which books you want your children to read on their own. Many times older siblings can be a great help in teaching the younger ones and will have lots of great ideas for projects. (One of the nice things about unit studies is it keeps the family together!) Remember, unit studies have the goal of tying in as many subjects as possible, so you don't need to supplement with a spelling workbook or vocabulary workbook unless your child has a definite need that can't be met any other way. Consider that it might be overloading the kids with work and creating frustration when they can't get it all done. (We speak from experience!)

How do I test to find out if my children have learned what I am teaching with the unit approach?

We have found that working closely with our children tells us all we need to know about what they comprehend and what they have not. By reading materials orally and then verbally questioning them, we know what needs review and what doesn't. They do many hands on activities that reinforce previously read materials. For example, in *Creation Science: A Study Guide to Creation!* there is a discussion on evolutionary principles. One of the points made is how evolution violates the second law of thermodynamics. That in itself sounds very dry and scholarly, yet a follow-up activity presented after the discussion is the Entropy Experiment which is a visual way to reinforce what they have learned. If the children can explain it to you, then you know they understand the concept. After reading all this, if you feel the need to create tests to find out what they know, feel free to do so! You could easily generate oral tests for the little ones, and essay questions for the older ones. One of the great things about homeschooling is the freedom to teach as you wish.

What about cooperative learning (co-ops)?

Cooperative learning (co-ops) is teaching a unit study with another family (or several families) and taking time once a week, or more, to work together on projects, experiments or activities for the entire day. Each family focuses on the unit materials at home during the week, and the co-op is a way of reinforcing the subjects taught at home. This unit lends itself well to co-ops. There are many experiments that would be fun to do as a group. Still, they can be done just as easily with a single family. The choice is yours.

Why teach using a science approach rather than literature or history?
     Each of the approaches have their pro's and con's. Without getting into all the reasons for focusing on science let us say it is a personal preference. We like science because it focuses on experimenting, which encourages creative thinking and exploration on a greater scale than either literature or history. Truly, it is a matter of preference.

SECTION 1: TEACHER CONTENT

Teaching Text Outline

Outline Background & Content

Teaching Outline

Teaching Outline

*Note: The words in **boldface** are defined in the glossary at the end of the book.

I. BODY ANALOGY — 1 Cor. 12:12-27

God uses the analogy of the Body of Christ to the human body. The Scripture in 1 Cor. 12:12-27 is beautifully written to show the dependence and inter-relatedness of the body and the unity He wants to see in His Church.

The Price of a Human Body — I have read various breakdowns of the value of the elemental minerals and the various components of the human body. Since the body is mostly water, some scientists have given its components a value of just a few dollars. Others have estimated that since the cost of everything has risen quite high lately, the elements in a body could be worth a million dollars. One biochemical company estimated that the ingredients (elements) needed to make up one human body would be worth $3,563,590.70. (Seuling 1986) However, the body does not operate merely at the elemental or atomic level. The human body functions at the molecular level. That means the body uses molecules, which are combinations of atoms, for proper function. For instance, instead of just using carbon, hydrogen, iron, oxygen, sulfur and nitrogen independently, our bodies use the largest, most complex molecule that occurs in nature — hemoglobin!

There are many other compounds like this that are needed for the body to function. (Red River of Life) Chemical compounds like this are tremendously expensive. In fact, the actual cost of these molecular compounds, if you could buy them, would make the human body priceless. Most compounds cannot be made synthetically. There is no biochemical company in existence that could put together all the molecular compounds necessary to make life function. But, if you could get the best pharmaceutical companies in the world to make the molecular compounds, there would not be enough money in the entire world to buy them. Even if you took into account all the money, all the gold reserves of all the countries, all the coal and oil still in the ground, all the lumber still in the forests and all the gold, diamonds and other precious gems still in the ground, there would not be enough money to buy the necessary ingredients for one human body! (McMurtry 1994) That makes each human PRICELESS. So many people today think human life is worthless. Babies are aborted, old people are euthanized and families are murdered for a few dollars.

The human body is priceless. However, that price has already been paid by The Only One who could ever pay the price: JESUS. He paid the price for the redemption of our sins by sacrificing Himself on the cross. His sacrifice allows us the privilege of living with Him in heaven for eternity.

COMMUNION

All different kinds of churches, synagogues and denominations celebrate the sacrifice of Our Lord in different ways. My church (Jill's) partakes of the emblems (symbolic ceremony 1 Cor 11:23-33) once a month. Felice's church celebrates Communion every Sunday during Mass. (Her Church teaches, and she believes Communion is the true presence: Body, Blood, Soul and Divinity of Jesus Christ: Luke 22:7-20, Mt. 26:17-29, Mark 14:12-25, 1 Cor 11:23-32) The Messianic Jews remember the Lord's death until He comes again at every Passover celebration. By whatever method your particular faith celebrates the Lord's Sacrifice, it is important to remember that we are all the Body of Christ and to participate with an awesome reverence for what Jesus Christ Our Lord has done.

The next time you are partaking of Communion, Eucharist, or Passover, stop and think. We must consider, each time, exactly what Jesus did for us. We must not eat and drink unworthily. The Last Supper was a Passover meal which Jesus was celebrating with His disciples. This same meal is repeated in Jewish homes every year to remember how God delivered the Hebrews out of the bondage they had suffered under Pharaoh in Egypt. As He passed around the unleavened bread, Jesus told His disciples to take and eat. "This is my body that is broken for you." In my church, we use the Jewish matzoh bread. In the process of preparing this bread (actually more like a cracker), it is pierced many times with a fork, and it is baked so that the bread comes striped. Therefore, the bread we partake of is pierced and striped like the Body of Christ. The next time you receive communion, hold it in your mouth for a moment and notice how the bread begins to taste sweet. This pierced and striped cracker, or bread, or wafer, becomes sweet tasting on the tongue, just as the sacrifice that Jesus made when His Body was broken becomes so very sweet in our lives.

The Last Supper was a Passover celebration, which the Jews call a Seder. Seder means 'set in order' or 'orderly.' Everything is done in a very precise manner according to Jewish tradition. If you have the opportunity to attend a Seder put on by the Jews for Jesus or a Messianic Synagogue, I would highly recommend it. Many of the symbolic elements in this meal point to Jesus as the Messiah. For instance, a piece of matzoh bread is broken into three parts, symbolizing the Father, Son, and Holy Spirit. Then the middle piece, the part that represents The Son, is wrapped in a white linen napkin and hidden in a high place. This represents the burial of Jesus. There is so much more involved in this meal: the bitter herbs, the roasted meat, and so on that all have important meanings.

Four cups of wine are used during this meal. The first cup is called the Cup of Sanctification; the second cup is the Cup of Judgment; the third cup is the Cup of Salvation. It was this third cup, the Cup of Salvation, that Jesus passed around to the disciples. As He passed this cup, Jesus told them that this emblem was His Blood that was shed for the remission of sins. As you partake of communion, consider how the Blood of Jesus washes away the sins in our lives. Jesus did not drink of the fourth cup, the Cup of Redemption, and He will not drink of it until He comes again. He did not even drink the wine mixed with water while He was on the cross. (This information came from a personal conversation with Steve Birnstien of the Beth Shiloh Messianic Synagogue of Ft. Myers 1996.)

Study the beautiful symbolism of the Seder meal that the Jewish people practice every Passover. This information is available online through Jews for Jesus.

The Bible puts a great deal of importance on the body and the blood, and on the

Body and the Blood of Christ. We must always remember that all believers are part of the Body of Christ, regardless of what doors of what building they may walk through to worship. When we get to Heaven, we won't be known by denomination or religion, but as heirs of the Kingdom.

II. BLOOD — HEART — RESPIRATION

The Circulatory System:
"...the life of every creature is its blood." (Leviticus 17:4)
"...the blood is the life." (Deuteronomy 12:23)

Blood is the most amazing transportation system ever devised. Small, flexible tubes called arteries and veins carry blood cells to and from the cells delivering oxygen and removing waste. Plasma is a fluid that carries those red blood cells as well as platelets that repair injuries, and white cells that fight infections. Blood is a modified connective tissue that acts as an amazing chemical plant that turns food into flesh, blood, bones and teeth.

The average person knows very little about how his own body works. The typical person probably knows more about the different fluids in the family car than about the various fluids in his own body. There are approximately seventy-five trillion cells in the human body, each having the same requirements. These cells must breathe, requiring oxygen; "burn" fuel, which requires a fuel source; get hot, and need cooling; perform work, and give off exhaust gas. Each one of these cells must be continuously supplied with oxygen and nutrients and have waste, gas, and water removed throughout a person's entire life. Unlike the automotive engine, which has separate systems for each function, God has combined these separate functions into one system, the circulatory system. Blood is truly amazing with sugar, fat, other chemicals and minerals that are constantly moving from processing sites to delivery points, taking waste material from cells to disposal plants, surrounding invading foreign material, then destroying them and replacing worn out or damaged parts. All this processing is controlled by electrical impulses from the brain, which is the central computing system.

As a car requires petroleum products on which to run, so the body requires fuel in the form of food. Cars use about 9,000 gallons of air for each gallon of gas. The body uses four gallons of oxygen per hour when at rest and seventy-five gallons of oxygen per hour when active. This oxygen must go from the lungs to every cell of the body very rapidly, and this is accomplished by the blood stream. (*Red River of Life*) We breathe air into our lungs, but we only use one/fifth of this air. Oxygen in the air is absorbed into the bloodstream by a physical process called **diffusion**. Gas bubbles in the blood would be fatal. Oxygen bonds to the hemoglobin molecule and is carried to the cells needing oxygen. The blood carries oxygen chiefly as an unstable compound which is formed in the lungs and which decomposes into oxygen and hemoglobin in the tissues. Hemoglobin is the largest, most complex molecule that occurs in nature:

$$C_{3032}H_{4812}N_{780}Fe_4O_{872}S_{12}$$

Our life depends on the four iron atoms that are protected by this giant molecule. When the oxygen reaches a cell in the big toe, it diffuses into the cell. At that same moment, the blood performs another vital function. It carries the exhaust gases from the cell. Exhaust gas from tissue cells is carbon dioxide (CO_2). The carbon dioxide is hydrated (combined with water) to form carbonic acid. Blood cells cannot tolerate carbonic acid; therefore, it must be neutralized instantly. After the acid is neutralized, the red cell takes it into the bloodstream where it combines with salt and plasma to form sodium bicarbonate (similar to ordinary baking soda, although we do not have white powdery stuff in our blood). This sodium bicarbonate is in a harmless form that is carried to the lungs.

However, when the blood carrying the waste product in this form reaches the lungs, another problem is encountered. Our lungs are not equipped to exhale waste products in this form. In the lungs the bicarbonate ions join with protons from hydrogen to form carbonic acid that begins to break down to form carbon dioxide gas and water just as it passes through the capillary wall to the lungs to be exhaled. At this same instant, the red cell picks up another load of fresh oxygen and begins another journey. Irwin L. Moon of the Moody Institute said, "To expect a red blood cell to do this is like asking a man to engrave the Lord's Prayer on the head of a pin as he passes that pin after being shot out of a cannon." (*Red River of Life*)

Just as the blood in our bodies is the source of our physical life, the precious Blood of Jesus gives us spiritual life. We are redeemed by the precious blood of Jesus. (1 Pet. 1:18-20) Lev. 17:11-14 says repeatedly that the life is in the blood. Heb. 10:4 tells us that the blood of animals cannot take away sins. Rom. 5:9-11 tells us that we are justified and reconciled to God through the blood of Jesus Christ.

**The blood of Jesus purifies us: 1John 1:7

**cleanses us: Heb 9:14

**is the source of new covenant: Heb. 12:24

**preserves and protects: Ex. 12:13

**reconciles and makes peace with God: Col. 1:20-22 **makes us holy: Heb. 13:12-15

**prepares and equips us: Heb. 13:20-21

**gives us the confidence to enter into God's presence: Heb. 10:19-22

**gives us the power to overcome the enemy: Rev. 12:11

It's all in the Blood, the Precious Blood of Jesus. Everything we need for a life of eternity with God is provided by the Blood.

The blood that gives us physical life gets around our bodies by a very special organ. The motor of the circulatory system is the heart, a fabulous two cylinder pump that is always working whether we are sleeping, sitting, mowing a lawn or running a race. This most important of muscles is about the size of our fist and it contracts and relaxes faster than once per second every day of every year of our life. The same blood moves continuously around the body, supplying the cells with oxygen and removing waste. If the flow of blood stops, the body dies within a few minutes. The heart, arteries, veins and capillaries make up the circulatory system. (Parker *The Heart and Blood* 1989)

An average adult body contains about 5.5 quarts (5 liters) of blood, which makes up about one-thirteenth of its weight. Every second the body makes 2.5 million new red blood cells. In about four months all red blood cells are replaced. A single red blood cell makes about 3,000 round trips through the circulatory system. (Seuling 1986) The heart weighs approximately 10 ounces (280 grams) and pumps 2.5 ounces of blood with each beat. The heart beats about 70 times each minute, which is how long it takes for blood to make one complete circulation around the body: 40 seconds in the body and 20 seconds to the lungs and back. This remarkable little pump moves 12 pints of blood through tens of thousands of miles of blood vessels every minute. (*Body Atlas 1995*)

There is even an ingenious system of valves and muscles that slows down the blood and reduces its pressure so that it doesn't explode the tiny capillaries. As the left ventricle squeezes blood through the aorta, the blood begins its journey under pressure. However, pressure and speed fall as the arteries branch and become smaller. The artery walls bulge with each heartbeat, then recoil to continue the work of squeezing the blood on its way. Therefore, this wonderful design takes the pressurized, jerky spurts of blood and smoothes them out so that when blood reaches the delicate capillaries, they are not damaged. This pump is so efficient that if it could be used for gasoline it could fill a large gasoline truck to overflowing in one day.

Our heart will pump blood around its system 3,400,000,000 times in 85 years. A pump crafted of the finest steel by the world's most skillful craftsman could not begin to match the endurance of the heart. (*Red River of Life*)

The heart is made of a special muscle, the cardiac muscle or **myocardium**, that never gets tired or fatigued like the muscles of the arms and legs, and is surrounded by a very thin, slippery membrane called the **pericardium**. The left side of the heart is twice as big as the right side because the left side pumps blood throughout the entire body, and the right side pumps blood to the lungs and back. The left side of the heart pumps bright, red blood that is rich in oxygen around the body. When the blood comes back to the heart, it is a dark bluish-red because the oxygen has been used up during its circuit and it has picked up the waste products. The right side of the heart then pumps the blood to the lungs where the waste goes out and fresh oxygen comes in, then back to the left side of the heart where it starts around the body again. The first organ to receive freshly oxygenated blood as it leaves the left ventricle is the heart itself via the two coronary arteries. Coronary comes from the Latin word *coronarius*, which means *"belonging to a wreath or crown"*, so called because the arteries encircle the top of the heart like a crown. (Parker *The Heart and Blood* 1989)

The highest blood pressure is of course in the left ventricle since the heart has to give it enough power to travel around the body. In the main artery the blood travels over 2.2 miles per hour (16 inches per second). The lowest blood pressure is in the right side of the heart where the blood comes in after its journey around the body. The slowest blood flow is in the tiny capillaries where the red blood cells move in single file at about 0.01 inches per second. At this rate, it is estimated that it would take a capillary one hundred years to fill up a cup. (Rowan 1995)

To understand how hard our heart is working, squeeze a tennis ball using both

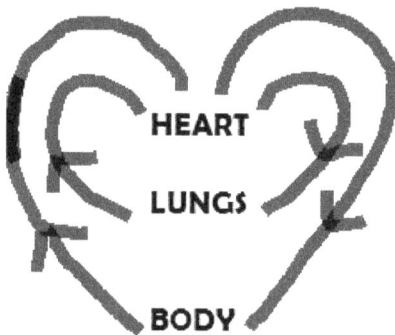

hands. This is about the same amount of force needed for the heart to pump blood out. Now squeeze the ball once per second for sixty seconds. Your hands will become very tired and maybe sore, but your heart can do this for our whole life without ever getting tired or stopping.

FACT —

Our first heartbeat occurred about the third week of pregnancy when we were about as big as the "C" in the word Child. (Rowan 1995)

Our circulatory system also contains veins that do the job of returning blood to the heart from all parts of our body. At any moment 3/4 of our blood supply is in the veins. On the return journey, the blood has lost a lot of its pressure, therefore, the veins do not have the same strains of pressure as the arteries. Vein walls are thin and pliable. To make up for changes in blood volume that can occur after serious bleeding, the largest veins can change their capacity by contracting muscles in their walls. (Parker *The Heart and Blood* 1989) Most larger veins have one-way valves to ensure that blood will continue to flow back to the heart. When a person is standing still, blood tends to collect in the feet, ankles and lower legs due to gravity. Walking and movement that uses the leg muscles squeezes veins and helps push blood back up to the heart. Standing straight for long periods may cause sentries or soldiers to faint from a shortage of blood in the brain.

The average capillary is 0.01 mm (0.0004 in.) wide. Most are less than 0.5mm (0.02 in.) long. Capillary walls are one cell thick, and blood travels through the capillaries at about 0.01 inch per second. So in about a second the blood has to exchange oxygen and nutrients for carbon dioxide and waste. The capillary network is so dense that few cells are very far from one. They are so narrow that a red blood cell actually has to squeeze through it.

FACT —

If all the blood vessels in the body were hooked together end to end they would measure over 90,000 miles (almost half way to the moon!). (Parker 1989)

Now, we will take a closer look at what is in the blood. Blood is very complex. Over half of blood is plasma, a yellow liquid containing nutrients, hormones and minerals. Red cells (**erythrocytes**) are extremely small, 0.007 millimeters (0.00028 inches) across. There are five million red cells in one cubic millimeter, which is about the size of a pinhead. Each red cell contains 270 million molecules of **hemoglobin** , which is a long protein chain that protects the very important iron portion . Red cells last about four months; then when they become old and can no longer carry enough oxygen, they are recycled in the liver and spleen. (Parker *The Heart and Blood* 1989)

One very interesting aspect of red blood cells is their shape, a bi-concave disk. Why aren't red cells shaped like a regular disk or a sphere? A sphere has a rapid absorption rate at first, but then it slows down substantially and it cannot absorb fast enough for the chemical reactions to occur. A simple disk has a rapid absorption rate, but not enough volume to satisfy the body's demands.

A group of scientists, intrigued by the shape of the red cells, fed a number of parameters into a computer to see what kind of results it would produce. Using calculus and the laws of gas fusion, they came up with the following equation:

$$\int^{\frac{\pi}{2}} \frac{dx}{\sqrt{1 - k^2 . \ sin^2 x}} = \frac{\pi}{2} \left[1 + \left(\frac{1}{2}\right) k4 + \left(\frac{1x3}{2x4}\right)^2 k^4 + \left(\frac{1x3x5}{2x4x6}\right) k^6 ... \right]$$

which the computer was then asked to draw. To their astonishment, the computer drew the cross section of a bi-concave disk, the exact shape of the cross-section of a red blood cell.

Cross-section of red cell:

 There is one perfect, ideal shape for chemical reactions to occur in red cells with enough speed and volume, and that is the one God gave to us. This shows that we were designed by an Intelligent Designer down to our tiniest parts. This would not be possible by random chance processes. (*Red River of Life*)

FACT — "The events of George Washington's death on Dec. 12, 1799 were recorded in the Virginia Medical Monthly. George Washington was suffering from a sore throat and fever. Since the doctor had not yet arrived, the overseer of the farm who was on hand began a blood-letting of one pint. After the doctors arrived there were two more copious bleedings. This was followed by another thirty-two ounce bleeding. At the last, the blood came slow and thick." (*Red River of Life*) This is made even more sad because there was a Bible lying on a table beside Washington's bed. Lev. 17:11 says, "for the life of the flesh is in the blood." There was no excuse for the doctors to bleed George Washington to death. He was probably just suffering from a cold and would have recovered.

 In about 120 A.D., a Greek medical writer named Galen believed that the heart, liver, and the brain gave the body life-giving spirits and made up blood that was used up by the body. In 1602, an Englishman named William Harvey became a doctor. He studied the human body for twenty years and disagreed with Galen. In 1628 he published a book entitled *An Anatomical Essay on the Movement of the Heart and Blood in Animals.* This was sixty-eight pages that changed medical science. Harvey recognized that the heart was a muscle and explained how the heart beat. He showed that blood moves in two circles through the body in a circulatory system, one to the lungs and one to the body using the same blood over and over. He also showed that the blood was moved by the action of the heart acting as a pump. (Yount 1994) Remember, "An anxious heart weighs a man down, but a kind word cheers him up." Proverbs 12:25.

 Blood is very important to our human life. It takes hormones, enzymes, nutrients and oxygen to every cell in our body. The endocrine system is made up of glands that produce various hormones, which are delivered by the circulatory system, that control the rhythms and functions of the body. The **thalamus** and the **hypothalamus** control hunger, thirst, sleep, body temperature and pituitary secretions. The pituitary gland controls the growth of the bones and regulates the other glands. The thyroid gland controls the development of the body and the rate of usage of the fuel in the body. The amount of calcium in the blood is regulated by the **parathyroid** glands. The **pineal gland** secretes melatonin and is involved with **circadian rhythms**. In children the **thymus** helps in the production of white cells that fight infection, but it apparently has no function in adults. The adrenal glands regulate the amount of salt and water in blood chemistry and produce adrenaline which gives the body extra power and energy in emergency situations. The pancreas produces insulin that controls the amount of blood sugar. Diabetics have to take an artificial source of insulin. (Guiness 1987)

There is power in our blood. The very special way in which it functions is crucial to life on Earth. In the same way, the Blood of Jesus is crucial to our eternal life. The Blood of Jesus gives us eternal life. There is Power in His Blood. Our blood cleans all of our tissues by removing waste products. Jesus paid the death penalty for our sins and His Blood cleanses us from all unrighteousness. The life of our flesh is in the blood which was perfectly designed by God. The life of our eternal spirit is in the Blood of Jesus which He lovingly shed for us. Remember, just as a doctor transfuses blood into people to give them life, we should be sharing the Blood of Jesus with people to give them eternal life. The Blood shall never lose its power.

RESPIRATION — "...and the Lord God formed man from the dust of the ground and breathed into his nostrils the breath of life, and man became a living being." (Genesis 2:7) Closely tied to the circulatory system is respiration. We rarely think about breathing even though we do it every few seconds. Breathing is essential for life, and being without oxygen for only a few minutes would be fatal. Every cell needs air as well as nutrients for biochemical reactions, turning food into energy and growing. The respiratory system consists of the nostrils, nasal cavities, mouth, throat (pharynx and larynx), windpipe (trachea), lungs and diaphragm. We breathe in air through our nose and mouth. Vital air travels down the windpipe to the lungs and into the bronchial tubes, bronchioles and into the tiny air sacs called alveoli. Each lung has 300 million alveoli. The movement of the diaphragm helps air flow into and out of the lungs. Oxygen is breathed in and is carried by the circulatory system to the body where waste carbon dioxide is collected and taken to the lungs to be breathed out.

The air we breathe in contains 78% nitrogen, 21% oxygen, 1% argon, 0.03% carbon dioxide and traces of other gases. We only use the oxygen. Each minute an adult breathes in 15-21 pints of air containing about four pints of oxygen. Each day an adult breathes in 530 cubic feet of air and each year would breathe in 275,000 tons of oxygen. Over an average lifetime of 500,000,000 breaths, a person would take in 14,000,000 cubic feet of air. (Parker *The Lungs and Breathing* 1989). These precious breaths come into two large, pink, spongy organs called the lungs. The right lung with its three lobes is larger than the left lung with two lobes. The heart is in between them. The trachea divides into **bronchi**, one for each lung, and these branch into **bronchioles** which branch smaller and smaller until they become the air sacs or **alveoli**. The walls of the alveoli are so thin that the oxygen passes through them into the red blood cells that are passing by. The **pleurae** are very slippery membranes that line the chest cavity and the lungs so that they move easily across each other. Just below the lungs is a large sheet of muscles called the diaphragm. This makes a wall between the lungs and the rest of the trunk. This large muscle tightens and relaxes as we breathe in and out. During quiet breathing it moves about 1/2" and about 2" during exercise. The ribs protect the lungs, and muscles between the ribs tighten and relax to allow the rib cage to move as we breathe. (Parker 1994)

But why do we need oxygen? The oxygen that is breathed in gets transported to the cell where it is "burned" with **glucose** to produce energy in a process called **metabolism**. Oxygen also combines with excess carbon to form carbon dioxide and water which are waste products. These waste products are then taken back to the lungs and breathed out. This process is know as cellular respiration, and the formula for what takes place is:

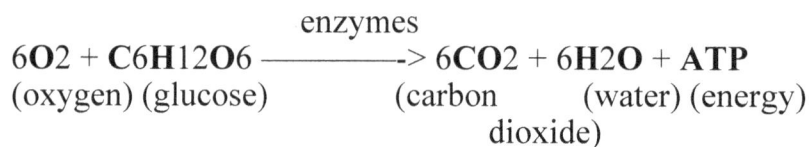

$$6O_2 + C_6H_{12}O_6 \xrightarrow{\text{enzymes}} 6CO_2 + 6H_2O + ATP$$

(oxygen) (glucose)   (carbon   (water) (energy)
dioxide)

Anyone who has ever gone skiing or hiking in the mountains knows that at about a mile high the air gets thinner and contains less oxygen. It becomes harder to breathe and we become tired more easily. Too little oxygen is harmful for the brain, although some people in the Andes Mountains have become accustomed to hiking in the mountains without harmful effects. Too much oxygen makes a person feel dizzy and faint.

The mechanics of breathing begin when a breath is taken in (inspiration) through the nose. The diaphragm tightens and moves down. The rib muscles tighten so the ribs move up and out thus making more room for the lungs that are now full of air. Then when we breathe out (expiration), the diaphragm relaxes and arches upward; then the rib muscles relax and move the rib cage down and in. This action helps to squeeze the water, carbon dioxide and the unused air out of the lungs. FACT: Adult lungs weigh about 2.2 pounds and hold about 6 quarts of air. (Caselli 1987)

A normal breathing rate is about twelve times per minute at rest. When exercising the rate is about eighty times per minute. The faster breathing is for the lungs to take in more oxygen which is required to produce more energy for the activity. The breathing rate adjusts automatically to meet the body's needs. An adult will breathe in about 2,200 gallons of air in twenty-four hours. (Parker 1994)

A person breathes in through the nose and sometimes the mouth (when one has nasal congestion or during vigorous activity). But the nose is the entrance and exit for the respiratory system. The palate is the floor of the nasal cavity and the roof of the mouth, and is important in making sounds. The nose has a special job to do in breathing to prepare the incoming air. Dust particles are filtered and trapped by hairs in the nostrils and by the mucous membrane. The extra supply of blood in the nose warms up the air while water from the lining of the nasal cavity moisturizes the air. This insures that the lungs receive filtered, warm, moist air which helps them work more effectively. (Parker 1989)

I have been out walking in winter in the dry climate of Denver and have experienced pain in my lungs when breathing in that cold, dry air too fast. God's design of the nose is absolutely perfect for helping the lungs with respiration.

Normally we do not think too much about breathing, but breathing can be controlled somewhat. A breath can be consciously held for a short time. Even a small child can take in a large breath hold it right before letting go with a loud cry. We can control the way we breathe when we talk, sing, speak loudly, or play a musical instrument. Deep breathing takes in more oxygen and gets rid of more carbon dioxide. Good posture can improve breathing, but we can only hold a breath for so long because the body's automatic response will cause the lungs to inhale a breath. God has built in this automatic, life-saving response.

God has also designed the lungs to be self-cleaning. A sticky mucous forms a layer on the lining of the airway and cilia (hairs) move back and forth to move the mucous with the trapped dust particles up and out of the lungs to prevent the alveoli from becoming clogged. The mucous is then swallowed and disposed of by the digestive system and we are probably not even aware of it. We also breathe in germs which the white cells in the alveoli destroy by digesting them. (LeVay 1993)

A problem of this century is air pollution, and breathing it in can be very hazardous to the body. There have been several killer smogs around the world. If there are too many particulates (solids in the air from dust or smoke) and/or carbon monoxide in the air, the lungs cannot function properly. Particulates, produced from wood-burning stoves and industrial smokestacks, can cause respiratory problems. The red blood cells will take up the carbon monoxide instead of oxygen and the cells will die, and under extreme conditions it could eventually result in the death of the body. Smoking causes the cilia to stop functioning properly and then mucous and dirt build up in the lungs. Smokers usually have difficulty breathing and have a characteristic "smoker's cough". (*Body Works 1995*)

Another important function of the respiratory system is the human voice and speech that is unique to our species. When air moves through the windpipe and over the vocal cords, sounds can be made. Air vibrates (moves) the cords making sounds. When the muscles stretch the vocal cords, the sounds become higher. Changing the position of the tongue and mouth turns the sounds into words. The voice box, or larynx, is made up of pieces of cartilage held together by muscles. The largest cartilage is called the thyroid cartilage and becomes larger in a boy when he reaches puberty, causing his voice to be come lower and may create a bulge in his neck called the 'Adam's apple'. The vocal cords are folds of mucous membrane that are stretched over the opening. Longer ones in males make a deeper voice and shorter ones in females make a higher voice. When a person is not talking, air passes over the vocal cords without making any noise. The gap between the cords is called the glottis. During normal speech. muscles tighten, pulling the cords together and air from the lungs vibrates them. Tightening or loosening of the muscles in the larynx, along with the mouth shape, produces different sounds.

Humans make other interesting sounds, such as laughing or crying. To laugh, we take in a deep breath and let it out in short bursts. A yawn is an extra deep breath, usually when we need more oxygen and as a sign we need rest. A sigh is a long breath out. Sneezes or coughs are noisy blasts of air to get rid of something. A sneeze can have a one hundred mile per hour velocity. Hiccups are caused when the diaphragm tightens suddenly, causing us to take in a short gasp of air. The hiccing sound is made when the vocal cords snap shut. (Parker 1994) The longest hiccuping on record is by Charles Osborne and lasted sixty-nine years and five months. (Sandeman 1995) Sounds are created by the mouth making various shapes, the lips, teeth, pharynx, larynx, hard palate, soft palate, nose and nasal cavity. The brain controls the muscles that move everything, and it also interprets the sounds that are produced so we recognize them as words. (See Section X on Language)

III. INJURIES and HEALING

Blood is more than red cells and plasma. Many substances are contained in the plasma: nutrients, minerals, etc. Some very important ones are there to begin the repair process after an injury. Carried within the plasma are white cells (**leucocytes**) which are larger and less numerous than red cells. There are about 10,000 of them in a cubic milliliter of blood. White cells fight disease. A white cell with a grainy texture is called a **granulocyte**. They engulf foreign substances and neutralize them. Other white cells are **lymphocytes** and **monocytes**. Platelets (**thrombocytes**) are 1/4 the size of a red cell. Although they live for less than two weeks and are not a true cell, but rather a fragment, platelets are very important because they are essential in helping the blood to clot after an injury. A clot is called a **thrombus**. **Platelets, fibrinogen, antigens, lymphocytes** and **antibodies** are all parts of the plasma contained in the blood that take part in repairing injuries. In fact plasma makes up 55% of the blood. (Engel-Ariele 1994)

Platelets help the blood to clot after an injury. They start a complicated series of chemical reactions at the location of the injury. Blood normally travels steadily through healthy vessels. When a vessel is injured, blood leaks out and damaged cells release chemicals that react with other chemicals in the plasma called clotting factors. There is a dissolved protein in plasma called fibrinogen that quickly converts to fibrin which is the insoluble, or solid form. Fibrin is long, sticky, yellow threads that form a mesh network that traps blood cells and platelets to seal the break. In a short while the fibrin threads will shorten, pulling the area into a firm mass called a thrombus or clot. This mass seals the injury, preventing blood from leaking away, and allowing the vessel wall to begin healing. When the injury is on the skin and is exposed to air, a scab forms to protect the wound. In a book entitled, *Darwin's Black Box* written by Michael Behe (who believes in the millions of years associated with Theistic evolution and makes it clear that he is not a Biblical Creationist) the clotting process is described as being so complex that it reflects intelligent Design. (Behe 1996) This is an outstanding admission because design implies a Designer and we know Who the Great Designer is. The Almighty God, Creator of Heaven and Earth, Who designed and created everything in six days, not millions of years.

Other cells in the blood are there to fight off infections caused by viruses or bacteria which we call "germs". These infecting bacteria and viruses can be breathed in or can enter through cuts and scrapes on the skin and will multiply rapidly. The wonderfully amazing white cells within our blood are designed to fight these infections. White cells known as neutrophils, eosinophils and monocytes "eat" invading germs through the process of **phagocytosis**. These white cells flow around the germs engulfing them. Chemicals then digest the germs. The inflammation and fever we feel when sickness occurs is caused by other types of white cells doing their job. **Basophils** and lymphocytes release chemicals that cause inflammation. The body has its own automatic thermostat that maintains a constant temperature except when the body requires a higher temperature to fight disease. (Brunn and Brunn 1982)

Some lymphocytes have special abilities. They can recognize the chemical patterns on germs called **antigens**. These lymphocytes then make **antibodies** that are specifically designed to attack those particular germs. Normally the white cells win the battle with the germs and the infection is over. But some lymphocytes will remember those germs and they remember how to make the specific antibodies needed to fight them. So if those bacteria or viruses enter the body again, the white cells recognize them and attack them before they have a chance to multiply. When this happens, we will not get sick and our bodies are "immune" to that particular infection.

Sometimes a doctor will deliberately inject some dead or weakened germs into our bodies in order to cause the white cells to manufacture antibodies. These germs do not generally make us sick, but our bodies will now know how to make antibodies should they invade again. A doctor calls this an immunization, and we usually have them as children.

Another important part of the body's defense system against infection is the lymph system. Lymph is a clear liquid that leaks into tissues from the plasma and is collected in its own system of vessels know as the lymph system. Lymph nodes are enlargements of lymph vessels and are not true glands. Lymph nodes swell when an infection occurs because the lymphocytes, the white cells that remember germs, are contained in these nodes and they begin to multiply in order to fight the infection. The spleen is another part of the lymph system and contains the type of white cells (phagocytes) that eat the germs. They also recycle old red cells and platelets. The spleen is about five inches long and is located behind the stomach. In babies, the spleen produces red and white cells, but in an adult, the bone marrow makes the majority of the red cells, so the spleen can be removed in an adult if it is damaged. (A.D.A.M. 1996)

Around 460 B.C., a Greek named Hippocrates moved medicine away from the realm of magic and superstition toward modern medicine. He thought that patients should be observed and accurate records of their conditions should be kept. He used very gentle methods to encourage natural healing. Through his observation, he identified and described many diseases. An Italian named Galen tried to explain every organ of the body but got them all wrong. Anton Von Leeuwenhoek was a Dutch drapier who made crude microscopes on the side. He is credited with making the first scientific observation through a microscope and was the first to draw pictures of protozoa. (*Grolier New Book of Knowledge*, s.v. "History of Science" and "Medicine".) See Section XII on Human History and Invention to see many Christian men of science.

In the book of Leviticus, God commands His people to stay away from each other for one week after handling the dead. They are considered to be unclean. The Center for Disease Control (the CDC) came out with a statement that one week is the time for infectious diseases to show up in a person who has handled a dead body and has made a recommendation for such people to be isolated for one week. Science catches up with the Bible. Also, health scientists have now decided that the human body needs one day a week to rest, and this rest is required for the body to remain healthy. Leviticus 23 tells us to work for six days and rest on the Sabbath. Science catches up with the Bible.

In Canada, doctors in twelve hospitals have opened Laughter Rooms because they believe that laughter is good for people, and it helps them to recover more quickly from illness and surgery. The Bible tells us that "A cheerful heart is good medicine." (Proverbs 17:22) Science catches up with the Bible once again. These scientists think that they have discovered something new for us, but anyone who studies the Bible knows that God, in His awesome wisdom, has always told His people how to live and what is best for them, not only for their physical bodies but also for their spirits. Proverbs 3:7-8 states, "...fear the Lord and shun evil. This will bring health to your body and nourishment to your bones." We should make sure we say something nice to someone today, for Proverbs 16:24 says, "Pleasant words are a honeycomb, sweet to the soul and healing to the bones."

IV. SKELETAL SYSTEM and MUSCLES

Our bones, the skeleton, are our framework. They give attachment to the muscles that allow us to move. Without muscles the body could not move, but without the skeleton, the muscles wouldn't have a way to contract and extend. The bones in the body do not make up a dead skeleton. Bones are alive. Biologists call the skeleton "dynamic". Just as a coral reef may look like a big rock but is actually a colony of living animals, so too, the bones are not dry sticks but are made of living cells that need food, give off waste, grow and repair themselves. (Rowan 1995) The rigid part of the bone has thousands of holes and tunnels for nerves and blood vessels. The bone is a hollow cylinder filled with a soft, fatty, gelatinous material called bone marrow. The blood cells are made in this red marrow that is about 70% fat. The bone is covered with a thin layer of specialized connective tissue called the **periosteum** that is involved with the healing of fractures.

The human body is a remarkable masterpiece of engineering and design. As Job writes in chapter ten verses 8-11, " Your hands shaped me and made me... Remember that you molded me like clay...Did you not...clothe me with skin and flesh and knit me together with bones and sinews?" This package is amazing for its strength, capabilities, efficiency of its processes, and it's all within a compact, flexible container. Bones are strong yet light. Pound for pound, the thigh bone is stronger than an equal weight of concrete. The 206 bones that make up the skeletal framework, support about 650 muscles plus all the organs which weigh about five times more than the bones. Very impressive engineering. The eighty bones of the skull, spine, and rib cage make up what is called the "axial skeleton". The rest of the bones are called the "appendicular skeleton". Check out this interesting fact: the distance inside the elbow to the wrist is just about the length of your foot. (Seuling 1986) The structure of the calcium and phosphorus atoms is a dense crystalline structure that give the bones their strength. (Daniels 1992)

The bones are more than a framework for movement and muscles. They also make the red blood cells which carry oxygen to all the cells, the white cells that fight off infection, and the platelets that release factors involved with the formation of clots. Even flat bones, such as the skull bones and the ribs, produce red blood cells. Bones also grow and repair themselves. Babies are born with 350 soft bones. As the child grows, the bones harden and many of them fuse together so that an adult has 206 bones. Bones grow by a process of new growth and reabsorption. Cells called **osteoblasts** deposit newly formed tissue in the form of osteocytes that harden into bone, while at the same time, **osteoclasts** dissolve and reabsorb bone tissue. The really neat thing about this system is that the osteoblasts make new bone faster than the osteoclasts dissolve old bone; therefore, the bones retain their basic shape as they get bigger. Another example of what a fabulous Engineer God is!

Bones have another function: they protect the vital organs. The skull protects the brain; ribs protect the heart and lungs. If you have ever been hit around the eye, you can appreciate why the eyes are recessed into the bone socket. Also, unlike the stiffly moving joints of a robot, the human body is very smooth and graceful in its movement. A runner's movement is as fluid and efficient as a graceful ballet dancer. An artist can put beautiful images on a canvas. An author can write stories with pen and paper or type on a keyboard with precisely controlled movement of the bones and muscles. Muscles are connected to the bones and held together at the joints by ligaments and tendons. The bones are moved by pairs of muscles. Muscles work in pairs because they can only exert force by contracting. Most movements require at least two muscles that work in opposition. For example, for the arm to bend, the triceps and biceps must work in opposition. The muscles on the inside of the arm must contract while the outer muscles must relax. Then to straighten the arm, the outside muscles must contract while the inside muscles relax. Muscles that cause joints to bend are called **flexors,** and muscles that straighten joints are called **extensors.** Energy is required for a muscle to contract, and that energy comes from nutrients in our food. This energy is stored as a special chemical called adenosine triphosphate (ATP) and is released when a nerve sends a message for a muscle to contract. When energy is needed, a chemical reaction takes place that breaks down the ATP into adenosine diphosphate (ADP) and a phosphate ion plus energy. Some of the energy is used to contract the muscle and the rest is given off as heat. (Daniels 1992)

The skeleton is flexible, not rigid, because the bones are connected at joints, locations where ends of bones meet. There are many types of joints; some are moveable and some are not. Some are hinges like the knee and elbow. Ball and socket joints, like the hips and shoulders, allow a large range of motion in most directions. Saddle joints, like the thumb or ankle, also allow a wide range of motion. Inside the joints is a slippery lubricant called the synovial fluid (after the Greek word for egg white) which the body manufactures in just the right grade and the right amount for each joint. Ligaments are strong bands of tissue that hold the bones together without stretching. Muscles end in a tough tissue called the tendons which connect the muscles to the bones.

Non-moving joints are mostly in the skull. The most moveable joint is the shoulder. The bone most often broken is the clavicle. The largest group of bones and joints are in the hands and feet. The smallest bones are in the middle ear and are smaller than a grain of rice. The smallest joint is between the stapes and the incus of the middle ear. The largest bone is the femur. The most complex joint is the knee. The largest bone without a joint is the patella (kneecap). The strongest bone in the head is the mandible (jawbone). The atlas and axis are specialized vertebrae that permit a wider range of motion than other vertebrae. The only bone not attached to any other is the hyoid bone in the floor on the mouth. The strongest joint is the hip joint and the strongest ligament is the iliofemoral at the hip joint. (Rowan 1995)

Muscles get their name from the Latin word for mouse, "musculus". Doctors, when looking at the function of muscles under the skin, said that it looked like a mouse under there. Muscles are always in use. Most of them are under our control, about 650 voluntary muscles. Involuntary muscles work without thinking about them, such as the heart, digestive organs and lungs and diaphragm, which is a good thing or else we would die the first time you fell asleep.

There are three types of muscles: striped or striated, which are voluntary muscles, that is, ones we can control that usually move the bones; smooth muscles, which are involuntary muscles that control the internal organs, digestion and the blood vessels; and cardiac muscle, which has some stripes but they are farther apart than in the striped muscle and this one is involuntary; we do not have to think about our heart rate. When a person is at rest, the heart rate slows down, and during activity, the heart rate increases without a conscious thought. Skeletal muscles are under our control. If we try to stand still for a while, our muscles tighten and flex to keep us standing erect. The muscles are moving the frame with thousands of complicated, intricate movements to maintain the standing position. This voluntary control over skeletal muscles allows a person to play the piano or violin, paint a waterfall, rollerblade down the street, or play a fast-paced game of basketball. Skeletal muscles are bundles of cylindrical fibers which contain even smaller fibers called myofibrils all under the control of nerve impulses that flow to and from the brain, which is the central processing unit, and all working together smoothly. (Guiness 1987)

These striped muscles can move so smoothly because they are attached to special joints that help with the movement. There are several different types of joints. The elbow and the knee are hinge joints (or ginglymus) and work similar to a door hinge (flexion, extension, and with the knee there is some movement in and out). The ankle joint is also a hinge or ginglymus, but the hinge looks like two saddles, one upside down on top of the other. The movement is flexion and extension, and because this joint bears the weight of the entire body, it can be easily strained or sprained. The hips and shoulders get their wide range of rotation from their ball-and-socket joints (or enarthrodial). The wrist is a radio-carpal joint (or condyloid articulation). The small bones of the wrist together form a smooth, convex surface called the **condyle**, which fits into a concave area formed by the end of the arm bone, the radius. The wrist has a wide range of motion: up and down (flexion and extension); side to side (abduction and adduction); and slight circular motion with the help of other joints (circumduction). (Gray 1977)

Luigi Galvani, who lived from 1737 to 1798, was an Italian physician who was studying the nervous system and muscles. He was rather amazed when he made a dead frog's legs jump when he touched them with a device he made from a piece of brass and a piece of iron joined together. When he touched this instrument to the frog, the moisture in the frog's body completed a current of electricity that made the muscles twitch. Galvani knew that electricity made the muscles move, but he wrongly believed that the electricity came from the frog. However, he really started something, because

Alessandro Volta, born in 1745, became another Italian scientist who discovered the source of electricity. He discovered that when two different metals were touching with paper soaked in salt water between them, a positive voltage (named after Mr. Volta) would be produced in one metal and a negative voltage in the other and could send a current through a wire, or a muscle, that was connected to them. Volta put several disks of zinc, silver, and paper wet with salt water, in a stack and realized he had made a stronger source of electrical current. This stack became know as a voltaic pile. Then another fellow, an English scientist named Sir Humphrey Davy (1778-1829) got the idea of connecting several voltaic piles together to form a battery. Remember, this all started with Galvani playing around with frogs' legs. (*Grolier New Book of Knowledge.* s.v. "Galvani" and "Volta".)

Consider the hand. God has created us with these amazing appendages that work as wonderful precision tools. It is not clumsy like the hand of an ape or a chimp, but rather it is graceful and precise. Normally instruments are designed for one specific function, such as a screwdriver or shovel or hammer, but look at how many different ways the hand can do a wide variety of things! The hand can swing a sledge hammer or delicately guide a surgeon's scalpel. The hand can form a fist for a weapon or skillfully thread a needle for cross stitching and sewing. No machine has ever been built that can change from handling a thick, heavy rope to handling a fine thread. Yet the hand does both with just the right amount of pressure for each. The hand also adapts differently to different things. It will hold a fork differently than it holds a hammer or a shovel. We can easily button a shirt, but no machine is capable of doing what we take for granted. However when some scientist invents a machine that can perform one function of the hand, he is applauded and receives praise for his marvelous design. But God is not given credit for the marvelous design of the supremely diversely functional hands He has made. (*Anatomy Series* 1992)

Hands not only perform tasks, but can feel things with the help of the sensory nerves and the brain. Touching and feeling record volumes of information and a wealth of knowledge about our world. People who are blind can read with their fingertips as they touch small bumps that represent all the letters and numbers, a system developed by Louis Braille. The nerves in the fingertips 'see' the bumps as letters, and the brain puts them together as words. The brain controls the muscles that move the hand across the Braille page and feel the bumps. Other nerves send messages to the brain about what was just felt. (See section on the Nervous System). The brain, the muscles, the skeleton, the nerves, and the blood that supplies all these tissues all work together as one, just as the Body of Christ should all work together in harmony as one.

One of the other types of muscles is the smooth or involuntary muscle. This makes up the digestive system and forms the hollow tubes of the intestines. Smooth muscle is found in the esophagus and the gastrointestinal tract, in the trachea and bronchial tubes of the lungs, in most of the glands and organs, in the arteries, veins, and lymph system, and in the iris. Smooth muscle is made up of contactile fibre-cells that are in small bundles which are gathered into larger bundles held together by connective tissue. These muscles usually respond to mechanical stimulus and react more slowly than the voluntary muscles. (Daniels 1992)

The third type of muscle is the cardiac muscle, or myocardial, which looks like a combination of smooth and striated and combines properties of both kinds. Striated muscles move quickly and powerfully, but become tired. Smooth muscles work without tiring but move slowly. The cardiac muscle has the strength of the striped muscles and the tireless action of the smooth. The heart beats at a steady rate but that rate can change rapidly when needed. At rest the heart beats 60-80 times per minute and pumps 5-6 quarts of blood in that time. During mild exercise such as walking, the heart beats 100-120 times per minute pumping 7-8 quarts of blood. During strenuous exercise the heart rate goes up to 200 beats per minute and pumps 30 quarts. Incredible range for that little pump. See section on the Circulatory System. (Daniels 1992)

V. DIGESTIVE SYSTEM

We must eat to live, and everything we eat must be broken down into a form that is usable by the body. Digestion is the process that takes the apple or hamburger that is eaten and turns it into nutrients to fuel for the body. Energy from the sun radiates on the apple tree to make it grow. It also radiates on the grass that a cow eats. When we eat the apple or the hamburger, we are consuming the stored energy. Digestion begins in the mouth where teeth grind food and the chemicals in saliva, such as **amylase**, turns starches into sugars. When the food is swallowed down the esophagus and into the stomach, the enzyme pepsin in the gastric juices breaks down proteins. Other enzymes from the pancreas continue the process in the small intestine where most of the nutrients are absorbed. Fats move through the system unaffected until they reach the small intestine where bile from the liver breaks them down. As what is left passes through the large intestine, the water in the food is absorbed and the rest is excreted.

Saliva is produced in three sets of large salivary glands, the largest of which is the **parotid glands,** and several smaller salivary glands located around the mouth . When food enters the mouth, salivation begins, but it can also be triggered by smell, sight or even the thought of food. Saliva is mostly water plus **serous fluid** which breaks starch down into sugars. Saliva also makes food easier to swallow and keeps the mouth moist for talking. Teeth are required to grind the food particles into small enough pieces to mix with saliva. Babies are born without any teeth showing. Some civilizations feed babies with food that has been vigorously chewed by another person, usually the parent. Starting at about six months to two years, the baby's teeth, about twenty, will appear. Between the ages of six to twelve, the baby teeth begin to fall out and are replaced by larger, permanent teeth as the mouth grows. Adults have approximately thirty two teeth. Teeth have roots that go well below the gum line into the jawbone to hold them firmly in place. Teeth have different shapes for different functions. The front teeth are sharp for biting, and the back teeth are flattened and grooved for grinding and chewing. The enamel covering the teeth is the hardest material in the body. (Guiness 1987)

When the food is swallowed, the **epiglottis** closes over the trachea or windpipe and moves the food to the esophagus and on to the stomach. But, if startled while eating, food could accidentally go down the windpipe. When this happens the body responds by coughing to blow the food forcibly up out of the windpipe in an involuntary reflex action. (Daniels 1992)

It is through the food we eat that we get the nutrients, vitamins, minerals, sugars, fats, protein, etc. that our bodies need. In the Middle Ages, it was widely accepted by physicians that the only foods to eat were meat, potatoes, bread and cheese. Scientists of the day believed that vegetables were so fibrous that they were about as nutritious as eating wood, and that fruit was so watery, it had no nutritional value at all. Scientists have changed their minds quite a bit, and now we know that vegetables and fruit are very beneficial. (Wolf 1995) The original diet in Genesis was best. Read Genesis 1:29. (Emerson 1996)

When food enters the stomach, gastrin cells are stimulated to release gastrin, and the gastric juices (consisting of hydrochloric acid and enzymes) work on the food. The stomach itself is protected from being digested by a mucous lining. The stomach also loses and replaces 500,000 cells per minute, so any damaged cells are quickly replaced. After the stomach has worked on its contents for several hours, it is now in the form of a paste that gets passed through the **duodenum** to the small intestine.

The pancreas is located near the duodenum and delivers its digestive enzymes into the small intestine. The pancreas also secretes hormones into the blood to control blood sugars; these hormones are insulin and glucagon. The enzymes from the pancreas that break down food are trypsin and chymotrypin which break proteins into peptides; **amylase** which breaks starches into sugars; and lipase, which along with bile from the gall bladder, breaks down fats into fatty acids and glycerol. These nutrients are absorbed by the small intestines, which are eighteen to twenty-three feet long, and stored in the liver. The inside of the small intestine is covered with **villi,** tiny little projections that are covered by **epithelial cells** that absorb the nutrients. Each villus is covered with 5000 columnar cells, and each one of these has a thousand microvilli that produce **end enzymes** that match only one particular nutrient. So the nutrients are now in a very microscopic size to be absorbed and stored in the liver. (A.D.A.M. 1996 and Daniels 1992)

The liver is an incredible organ that performs over 500 different tasks. It stores carbohydrates, vitamins, and nutrients; disposes of old blood cells; makes protein; breaks down food; creates bile; and disposes of poisons by making them harmless. This is a very versatile and powerful organ. In fact the ancient Greeks thought it was the seat of emotions. When they loved someone they would say, "I love you with all my liver". (Seuling 1986) But an even more fantastic fact than this is that the liver can regenerate itself even if only 10% of the organ remains, and a small piece of liver can be transplanted from one person to another and it will grow into a complete organ. (Rowan 1995)

The last section of the digestive system is the large intestine. The job of this five foot long organ is to remove water and eliminate the waste matter from the body. The large intestine is made up of the **cecum**, the **colon** and the **rectum.** The moist paste (processed food) enters the cecum and peristaltic action forces the food stuff through the intestine squeezing the moisture out as it goes, and is finally excreted through the rectum. The whole process takes between twelve and twenty-five hours. (Daniels 1992)

The kidneys also process waste. Working with the ureters, the bladder, and the urethra, the kidneys are constantly filtering the blood and removing the waste products and balancing the blood's chemistry. The kidneys are as complex as the human brain! Kidneys are located on both sides of the spine and are about the size of a fist. Blood gets to the kidneys from the heart through the renal arteries (more than a quart per minute).

Blood is then filtered through **nephrons** within the kidneys, approximately one million in each. After being cleaned, most of the fluid is reabsorbed except for one percent that is waste material and is sent to the bladder. The cleaned blood is sent back to the heart by the renal veins. The waste products from the blood become the urine. Urine is stored in the bladder until expelled through the urethra. In a lifetime the kidneys can clean out more than one million gallons of water — enough to fill a small lake. (Daniels 1992)

The kidneys remove excess salt or water from the blood. They also keep concentrations of glucose, protein and body chemicals constant. Too much salt absorbs moisture and dries up the cells. That's why salty foods make us thirsty. Retaining too much fluid is also not good for the body. It can be seen that the work of the kidneys is not only important but vital. People whose kidneys have failed will have to have this filtering job done for them by a machine in a process called dialysis. (A.D.A.M. 1996) The digestive process can be diagrammed this way:

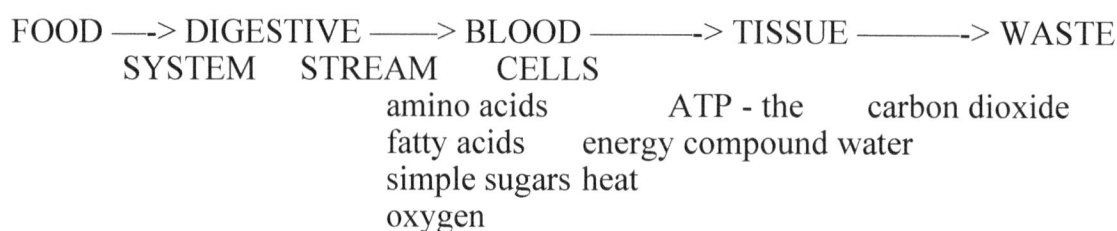

FOOD —-> DIGESTIVE ——> BLOOD ————-> TISSUE ————-> WASTE
           SYSTEM   STREAM   CELLS
                              amino acids   ATP - the   carbon dioxide
                              fatty acids   energy compound water
                              simple sugars heat
                              oxygen

There is one other very important thing we must digest, and that is The Word of God. Jesus is called the Bread of Life, and we should take Him into ourselves by studying God's Word. We are commanded to meditate on The Word. The word "'meditate" is the same root word that describes how a sheep ruminates its food. A sheep will eat and swallow, then regurgitate it and chew on it some more to get more nutrition from it. We should hide God's Word in our hearts and continually go over it, and we will get something new and beneficial from it every time.

VI. NERVOUS SYSTEM and BRAIN

The brain and the nervous system are the master control system for the body. They perform all functions of thinking, sleeping, feeling pain, breathing, moving, seeing, hearing, tasting, smelling, eating, secreting, growing, controlling temperature, receiving input from the senses, processing this information and formatting a response.

You can point to your brain, but you cannot point to your mind. Scientists can understand how some areas of the brain work, but do not understand the mind. Some scientists say that the workings of the mind fall outside the realm of science. Scientists can, however, understand that it is the brain that performs all the physical functions of the body, as well as thinking, learning, imagining, reasoning, dreaming, creating, feeling emotions and all other intellectual activities. We are aware of ourselves and our activities because of the brain. Scientists disagree as to whether or not animals are aware of themselves and their activities or whether they act totally on instinct. We have personality and creativity because of the brain. We are body, soul, and spirit. The soul is made up of the mind, will, and emotions.

The brain has been compared to a computer. However, this is not a very good comparison. A computer can only solve instructions one at a time even though it works at a very rapid rate. The brain processes millions of bits of information simultaneously. Both rely on electrical impulses. The brain operates on about the same amount of power as a ten watt bulb. (Seuling 1986) But the brain can analyze information, format a plan of action and even reprogram itself and make decisions. No computer can do these things. No artificial intelligence comes close to the brain; besides, some programmer with a "*brain*" has to tell the computer what to do. Computers cannot spontaneously laugh or love.

Recently, Garry Kasparov, the World Chess Champion, was pitted against a super computer named Deep Blue. Programmers gave the machine its chess skills but that does not mean it can think or reason. It merely uses its ability to manipulate millions of possibilities in a short time. Kasparov would use his reason and strategy skills to plan his next move, while Deep Blue would use only its many calculations. Asking a man to compete with a computer is like asking a weight-lifter to compete with a forklift. The machine could lift more weight but it is not a thinking machine. Deep Blue cannot think or reason and it has no conscience. Many computer programmers believe it has a soul and a conscience. Fortunately for all of us, Kasparov won the tournament.

Not real pretty to look at, the brain is eighty-five percent water and made up of pink and gray fatty matter composed of billions of nerve cells. Brain cells and muscle cells are the only cells in the body that are not replaced. (Seuling 1986) We have all the brain cells we will ever have as a baby. Under the gray matter is white matter made up of nerve fibers. The brain has three basic parts: the **cerebrum** composed of two halves, or hemispheres; the **cerebellum** which coordinates the movement of the muscles and maintains equilibrium by constantly calculating balance; and the **brain stem** which includes the thalamus, hypothalamus, pons, and medulla. The thalamus, hypothalamus and pituitary gland regulate hunger, thirst, sleep, body temperature and other behaviors. All messages to the brain, except smell, pass through here. The **cerebral cortex** is the covering that is the very outer portion of both cerebral hemispheres and contains intelligence. The **medulla** governs blood pressure, heart rate, breathing and other vital functions. The **corpus callous** links both sides of the brain so they work in unison. (Gray 1977)

The two halves of the brain are called the hemispheres. There is a dominant hemisphere and a non-dominant hemisphere. Ninety percent of people have the left side of the brain as the dominant hemisphere which controls reading, writing, reason, and math skills. These people are right-handed. Ten percent of all people have the right side of the brain as the dominant hemisphere and are left-handed. The two hemispheres of the cerebrum make up eighty-three percent of the weight of the brain. The lobes of the cerebral cortex have different jobs. The frontal lobe (in front) controls speech, behavior, and skilled movement. The temporal lobe (near the temple) is where hearing and smell are located. The parietal lobe (top rear) is the location of touch, vision and large movements. The occipital lobe (bottom rear) is another location for vision. The limbic system, which is located under the temporal lobe, is the control center for mood and memory. (A.D.A.M. 1996)

Although it is made up of neuron and nerve fibers, the brain itself has no pain receptors. The meninges are three layers of outer covering of the spinal cord and brain that are sensitive to pain and are where we feel headaches. Pia mater is the inner covering and carries blood vessels to the brain. The arachnoid is the middle layer. The outer layer is the dura mater and it is the toughest. (A.D.A.M. 1996)

A program I once viewed on The Learning Channel called "Ancient Man" was exploring why an ape would want to walk erect. All apes walk and run on four limbs, though they will stand on their hind limbs and even walk on them for short periods. But so do squirrels, chipmunks, ground hogs, and a host of other critters that are not assumed to be our ancestors.

Some of the scientists on the program said that there was no workable transition from quadra-pedalism to bi-pedalism. The entire hip and knee structure of apes would have to radically change to accommodate walking on two legs. That would be a logical assumption. However, other scientists on this program said that bi-pedalism is the result of hot weather on the savanna floor in Africa. I was amazed at this inductive reasoning, so I grabbed a pencil and started making notes.

According to one scientist, the temperature on the floor of the African savanna was so hot the the apes' brains needed cooling. Therefore, they stood up to reach the cooler air a few feet above the surface. Another scientist, who also agreed with this theory, said that the head and brain would have to have "very special plumbing", and the "creation" of the vertebral venus plexus for blood to flow up into the ape's brain for bi-pedal locomotion. Without this the apes would become dizzy and fall back to the savanna floor because they already have lower blood flow to their brains. There would have to be new skull configuration, new tunnels through the skull to accommodate the new blood vessels that would go to the new brain.

One scientist said that it would "take a lot of special plumbing" to achieve this change. Now, I presume that in any other subject area these people would have a normal intelligence, but when it comes to evolution they feel free to make wild, imaginative assumptions about changes in species. I wrote down this quote from one of the scientists, "The hot floor of the savanna required that the apes' brains needed cooling and therefore developed emissary veins in the cranium and holes in the skull, through which the veins would pass, in order for the apes to walk upright. This would allow them to overcome the thermal constraints and low blood flow that would hinder the growth of larger brains." Folks, please don't believe everything you hear on television. Much of it is nothing but science fiction. (*Ancient Man* 1995)

The nervous system is really two systems: the *central nervous system* and the *autonomic nervous system*. The brain, the spinal cord, the cranial nerves, the spinal nerves, and the **ganglia** make up the central nervous system, also called the cerebro-spinal system. The autonomic nervous system includes the sympathetic and parasympathetic systems. This system is a double set of ganglia that send and receive messages and are not directly connected to the brain, but are indirectly connected through the cranial and spinal nerves. A nerve is a bundle of axons, sort of like a telephone cable. A neuron is an **axon**, a dendrite and a nerve cell body. The nervous system has a lot of responsibility. It protects us from harm by quickly sending a message to the brain that something is harmful and then zipping a message from the brain to the body to move away from the harm. (Gray 1977) It takes about 1/50 of a second for a pain impulse from the big toe to reach the brain. (Seuling 1986) The nervous system maintains balance and tells us when we should sleep so the rest of us can rest. Some people, such as athletes, can even condition themselves to endure a lot of pain and injury. (Gray 1977)

Skin is absolutely wonderful! Not only is it a protective, semi-waterproof covering that is flexible, keeps out germs, regulates body temperature and keeps in moisture, it's loaded with neurons that make it sensitive to touch. We get input through the skin about the environment around us just like we do through our eyes and ears. The skin has two layers: the **epidermis** that you can see with its pores and hairs, and the **dermis**, the lower layer that contains the blood vessels, sweat glands, hair roots and the nerves; lots and lots of nerves.

In order to protect the body, the skin must be able to detect many sensations like pain, hot, cold, pressure, etc. The very outer layer, the epidermis, has no nerves. It is mostly dead skin cells waiting to flake off and be replaced from underneath. A pin can be stuck into this layer of dead skin without the sensation of pain. The dead skin scales off the epidermis at the rate of about five billion per day. The entire skin is replaced every twenty-eight days. In fact, most of the dust in your house consists of these skin scales. (*The Secret Life of 118 Green Street* 1995)

In the dermis, just below the outer layer are millions of receptors that can sense all these feelings. Isolating single sensation receptors is difficult since many of them occur together. Some receptors have been thought to receive different sensations and relay them to the brain. Free nerve endings and other nerves wrapped around the base of hairs register pain, heat, and touch. The spherical Pacinian corpuscles sense pressure. Touch and pressure are detected by the Ruffini endings and the Meissner's corpuscles. The sensation of cold apparently comes from the Krause end bulbs. (Guiness 1987)

Some areas of the skin are much more sensitive than others. The lips, tongue and fingertips are the most sensitive. The fingertips contain many more pain receptor nerves than other areas. Besides containing the pain receptors the skin on the fingertips forms a pattern of ridges called fingerprints. Each of our ten fingerprints are different. No two people in the world have identical fingerprints, not even identical twins. The shoulders, arms and thighs are the least sensitive. But how do we actually "feel" something? When we touch something, hot, cold, soft, or whatever, the sensory receptors in the skin send off an electrical current or nerve impulse that is chemically produced. The nerve impulse must cross over a gap or **synapse** to get to the next **neuron** in an **axon** terminal. The process is enhanced by chemicals called **neurotransmitters** that cause the impulse to go on to the next neuron. (Daniels 1992) There are periodic constrictions along the nerve sheath called Nodes of Ranvier that keep the impulse moving. Then the impulse enters a ganglion (bundles of **nerve** cell bodies) near the spine, then into the spinal cord and up to the gray matter in the brain. This is a one-way trip for this message, like a telegraph message sent over a wire. The return message from the brain, after it analyzes the information, goes to the efferent neurons that send messages to the muscles to properly respond.(A.D.A.M. 1996)

The sense of touch is not only valuable for the reasons stated, but doctors now believe that it is essential for babies to be held and touched and loved to ensure physical and emotional growth. Studies have shown that premature infants who only received regular hospital care did not thrive as well as those who were held and touched by the nurses. Touching is not only important to babies, but also people of all ages. Touching establishes feelings of well being. (Guiness 1987) One PBS program did a survey of people's response to tellers and clerks when they were gently and inconspicuously touched by the teller or clerk, and when they were not touched. The overall results were very interesting. The times when people were touched, they had a better feeling about the teller and the bank, or the clerk and the store. The times when the people were not touched, they had much less positive feelings for the service. (*Human Nature* 1995)

VII. REPRODUCTIVE SYSTEM

The smallest living thing is a virus (there is some argument as to whether or not viruses are alive) but a virus needs a living host in which to reproduce, so how could it have been the first living thing to evolve from primordial goop as some evolutionists believe? The next largest living thing is bacteria, but it too has a similar problem of needing a **substrate**. Even the so-called "simplest cell" is very complex. According to an evolutionist, J. Keosian, even the simplest cell "is an intricate...unit of harmoniously coordinated parts and chemical pathways. Its spontaneous assembly out of the environment, granting the unlikely simultaneous presence together of all the parts, is not a believable possibility." (Richards 1987) But still this evolutionist and others cling tenaciously to their belief. Why? Because the only alternative is Special Creation by a Divine Creator, and they don't want to believe there is a God. First Timothy 6:20-21 explains that with a warning: "Turn away from godless chatter and the opposing ideas of what is falsely called knowledge, which some have professed and in so doing have wandered from the faith".

Why is the spontaneous appearance of life out of non-living substance not a believable possibility? Because over twenty amino acids are needed to make up the proteins of living things. Nineteen have been reproduced chemically, but some very essential ones have never been reproduced (even with a whole lot of intelligence behind it trying very hard). Besides that, the heat used to make amino acids will destroy them. No environment on earth could ever have existed that could produce all kinds of amino acids necessary for life. This is another enigma for evolutionists.

Another problem evolutionists have is **porphyrin**, the essential molecule in hemoglobin that carries oxygen. Porphyrin had to have been around in the beginning for life to have begun and thrived because some chemicals of a cell are broken down by oxygen unless prophyrin is present. In other words, the porphyrin inhibits the oxygenation of some chemicals. Porphyrins can only be made where there is plenty of oxygen to be used. Now, consider that amino acids can only be produced in an environment where there is no oxygen present. (Richards 1987) This major problem for evolutionists is how these two essential chemicals could have ever been produced and come together in the same primordial soup. One requires oxygen to be present, the other requires that *no* oxygen be present. The Creationist has the answer: they were both created simultaneously in the living cell, which is the only place where they can exist together. Life from non-living substances... "It couldn't just happen". (Richards 1987)

34

So, how does life begin? The most incredible miracle of the human body is the development of new life. Each cell in the human body (except for red blood cells) has forty-six chromosomes, except for the egg and the sperm which have twenty-three each. Two of the forty-six chromosomes determine the gender of the new person, and others determine hair and eye color, bone structure, height, body chemistry, and all other inherited characteristics. Except for identical twins, no two people have the exact same DNA code in their chromosomes. (*Grolier New Book of Knowledge* s.v. "Chromosomes". 1982)

Y   y Parent Plants (second generation)

	Y	Y	y	
Parent	Y	YY	Yy	Offspring YY & Yy = yellow
Plants	y	Yy	yy	Offspring yy = green

This chart shows how genes from each parent would come together to produce possible offspring. This explained why Mendel observed that 3/4 of the seeds were yellow and 1/4 were green. He performed other experiments with plant height and flower color and this same 3:1 ratio of dominant to recessive traits was consistent. (*Grolier New Book of Knowledge* s.v. "Mendel") This same system determines all of our characteristics including whether or not we have hitchhiker's thumb, or how our ear lobes look, and whether or not we can roll our tongue. Genetics show us that there is a 50-50 probability that a new baby will be boy or a girl:

male
parent

	X	X	female parent
X	XX	XX	XX = female
Y	XY	XY	XY = male

There are many good books and videos available on sexual reproduction. As parents, we have the discretion to teach reproduction whenever we feel it is appropriate for our children. I will begin here with the fertilized egg. The sperm, with its twenty-three chromosomes combines with the ovum, or egg cell with its twenty-three chromosomes to make a complete set of forty-six chromosomes. Every human spends approximately half an hour as a single cell (Seuling 1986). The fertilized egg begins dividing and reproducing within twenty-four hours of the moment it was fertilized. The fertilized egg will divide five to six times as it travels to the uterus where it attaches and begins to grow. What started out as a single fertilized egg cell will become a newborn baby in just nine months with more than six trillion cells that make up its organs, bones, skin, blood, etc. While the baby is developing in the womb, it floats in the amniotic fluid of the amniotic sac which protects it. (Guiness 1987)

There are many firsts that occur after fertilization:

> In about 12 days — the brain is distinguishable from the rest of the baby
> 3 weeks — the first heartbeat
> 5-6 weeks — first bone hardens (ossifies)
> 7.5 weeks — knee and elbow joints
> 3rd month — first nail appears
> 4th month — first hair
> 5th month — mother feels first movement
> 6th month — eyes first open
> 8th month — baby responds to mother's voice
> 9th month — **Birth**, first breath
> 1st month after birth — recognizes Mom's smell
> 6 weeks — first smile
> 2-3 months — recognizes Mom's face
> 4th month — first laugh
> 5th month — rolls over for first time
> 6th month — begins to make sounds and crawl
> 9th month — says first word: now has control over breath, mouth,
> tongue, larynx, lips and brain.
> 9 months -1 year — first steps: now has control over a complicated
> system of muscle contractions to keep his center of gravity over the leg
> that is supporting the weight, coordinated by the cerebellum in the brain.
> (Rowan 1995)

Cells come in all shapes and sizes, and they are the basic units of which all people, plants and animals are made. Some plants and animals are one-celled organisms, others are multicellular, and people are extremely complex. An adult has around 75 trillion cells in his or her body. Smaller animals have fewer cells, larger animals have more. For instance, an elephant has eighty-five times the number of cells as we have. FACTS: The largest human cell is a megakaryocyte in bone marrow. The smallest human cell is a microglial cell in the brain. The cell with the shortest life is in the lining of the intestines which lasts three to four days. The cell with the longest life is the Purkinje cell of the brain synapses which lasts for life. (Rowan 1995 and *Nine Month Miracle* 1995)

Cells come together to form tissue, and tissues form organs. Most of the cell, about 70%, is water in the **cytoplasm,** a clear jelly-like substance in which all other cell parts float. The garbage collectors of the cell are the lysosomes which digest bacteria and worn out cell parts. Ribosomes assemble chains of amino acids into proteins or polypeptides. They attach to RNA strands to precisely reproduce all the various proteins. Protein is stored in the **golgi complex** until the cell needs it. DNA is made up of nucleotides that code for protein, but protein is made by the DNA, so which came first? Mitochondria is the powerhouse of the cells. The heart cells have ten times as much mitochondria as do muscles in the legs. Endoplasmic reticulum is the channels in which the cell material moves around. The center of the cell is the nucleus which contains the DNA with its chromosomes, which are made up of genes that carry the code for making proteins. (Rowan 1995)

Genetics is the study of genes and heredity, or how offspring resemble and differ from their parents. Gregor Johann Mendel (1822-1884) was an Austrian priest who did plant breeding with pea plants and studied the various kinds of offspring. Since Mendel kept very meticulous records of parents and offspring, he was able to work out the laws of heredity, also called the Laws of Genetics. Mendel's initial experiments crossed plants that produced only yellow seeds with plants that produced only green seeds. The first generation produced only yellow seeds. The second generation produced some yellow and some green seeds. He carefully recorded all the crossings with the second generation, and the results were over 6000 yellow seeds and over 2000 green seeds. Mendel concluded that since the first generation produced only yellow seeds that yellow was a dominant trait, and since the green reappeared in the next generation that green was a recessive trait. And since the number of dominant to recessive seeds was about 3:1, Mendel came up with the letter representation for the genes that is still used today. The following chart was developed by Mendel for the second generation plants: **YY** represents the dominant yellow trait and **yy** represents the recessive green.

Evolutionists have tried very hard to use DNA and chromosomes to prove that evolution is a fact by hypothesizing that more complex life forms should show more complexity. They tried to say that the length of the DNA strand should be longer with so-called higher life forms, but that proved to be wrong. The DNA strand of a starfish is one foot long; a pigeon's is two feet long; a human's is six feet long and a frog's DNA strand is eight feet long. DNA length is no proof of more complexity. Then evolutionists said that the number of chromosomes within the DNA would be higher in higher life forms, so they counted chromosomes. An ant has two, a bee has sixteen, a frog has twenty-six, a mouse has forty, a human has forty-six, a snail has fifty-four, a chicken has seventy-eight, and a fern, which is supposed to be a "primitive" plant, has 1260 chromosomes. The number of chromosomes is not consistent with higher life forms. (Rowan 1995)

A comparison of the amino acid sequences of Cytochrome C was thought to be the proof the evolutionist needed to prove their theory that higher life forms would have greater complexity. However, the comparison of Cytochrome C of several animals shows no hint of evolution. In fact, the difference between a single-celled bacteria and a horse is less than the difference between a single-celled bacteria and a single-celled yeast. This was quite a shock for the evolutionists to find no increasing complexity. (Bliss 1988)

In 1868, a fellow named Ernst Haeckel was so determined to prove evolution that he deliberately altered drawings of various animal embryos and a human embryo to make them look alike. These were drawings he had stolen from a colleague. Haeckel used these drawings to prove "ontology recapitulates phylogeny" which means that the embryonic cycle repeats a species' evolutionary history. The gills were from when we were fish, the yolk sac was from when we were birds, and the tail was from when we were monkeys. What Haeckel called gill slits have nothing to do with respiration in a developing baby. These are pharyngeal pouches of the embryo, and they develop into the middle ear canal, the parathyroid gland, and the thymus gland. What Haeckel called the yolk sac is actually the baby's blood-forming sac where its first blood cells are formed. This has nothing to do with nourishing the developing baby. Of course Haeckel lengthened the end of the spine to show that we had a tail. The last bone in the spine is the coccyx and was deliberately misnamed the "tail bone". This bone stimulates the growth of the legs. It is also the point of attachment for the muscles that allow humans to sit upright. We never had a tail! Any primate would have to change its entire hip structure and knee structure to accommodate sitting and walking upright. (Bliss 1988)

I think that perhaps the most distressing thing about Ernst Haeckle's fraudulent drawings was that they were proven to be false by one of his own colleagues, Wilhelm His, in 1874. Haeckle called this his biogenetic law. Even after he was "found out", Haeckel remained completely unrepentant about his falsifications. Yet, I was being taught this as a fact in college in 1972, a hundred years later. The lie of evolution was being perpetuated and I believed everything I was being taught. [Felice's Note: My daughter's friend's College Biology (2002) text still contained Haeckel's drawings. When she confronted the professor privately, the professor agreed it was false, however, made no attempt to mention it to the entire class. The question remains "Why does this drawing remain in current textbooks?" I believe the answer is obvious.]

VIII. DNA and the ORIGINS of LIFE

DNA stands for **deoxyribonucleic acid**. Amino acids make up proteins. A **nucleotide** is composed of a sugar, a phosphate and a nitrogenous base formed by dehydration synthesis. Dehydration means to remove water. Therefore, when a base sequence or codon (three letters that code for an amino acid) is formed it squeezes out a molecule of water to form a nucleotide. The nucleotide is defined by the sugars it contains. Those that contain the sugar ribose are called ribonucleotides which come together in long chains of from seventy-five to many thousands to form **ribonucleic acid** or RNA. Those that contain the sugar deoxyribose are called deoxyribonucleotides, and they come together in chains of many thousands to form deoxyribonucleic acid or DNA. The DNA molecule has two chains of nucleotides that wind around each other to form what is called the double helix.

The nucleus of each cell contains the DNA which carries all the hereditary information about the person. A gene is a DNA sequence that codes for a protein or polypeptide. In other words, a gene is a model or recipe for a protein. Each person gets half of his or her DNA (genes) from each parent. This requires that the two chains of the DNA double helix must split apart. This process ensures that the hereditary information is continually passed on to the next generation. The RNA is essential to this process of replication. This process is similar to making a plaster cast of a head. The cast is the reverse. This cast is then filled with some other material and produces a mold of the head that looks just like the original head. When the transfer RNA fits into the messenger RNA, then the DNA pattern of the right number of amino acids in the proper order is reproduced exactly. (*Grolier New Book of Knowledge* s.v. "DNA". 1982) This process of mitosis seems like a very complicated process to have evolved by chance over time.

Evolutionists believe that all living things have formed over long periods of time and multiple mutations from one single cell that formed accidentally by just the right amino acids coming together in just the right way in some "primordial soup" on this planet billions of years ago. N. Takahata of the Graduate University for Advanced Studies in Hayama, Japan, wrote the following in a paper on the molecular anthropology of hominid DNA sequences: "Even with the DNA sequence data, we have *NO* direct access to the processes of evolution, so objective reconstruction of the vanished past can be achieved only by *creative imagination*." (Takahata 1995) Creative imagination does not involve ANY science, because science involves that which is testable and observable and repeatable. After examining many of the hominid fossils and writing about when they first appeared, how long they lived and when they died out, Takahata says. "However, there are not enough fossil records to answer when, where, and how *Homo sapiens* emerged." (Takahata 1995) There are many problems with this theory, and what is observed in nature does not fit into the evolutionary theory either. The term "natural selection" was thought up by a Creation Scientist twenty-four years before Darwin. Natural selection is not the same as macroevolution. Natural selection tends to weed out mutation and discourage change and acts in favor of stasis (No change!). Darwinism became popular because Darwin took the general theory of evolution which had been around since the ancient Greeks and added natural selection to it as a means for change. Evolution means change, and natural selection discourages change. No transitional fossils have ever been discovered. Those fossils that were thought to be transitional have later been evaluated to be either another species or fakes.

There have been several deliberate hoaxes that some scientists have perpetrated on the public as "proof of evolution". Piltdown Man is a famous example. Two teachers combined a human skull with an ape jaw that had been altered and had the jaw and teeth filed down. They then buried it near the town of Piltdown and had a class of students "discover" it two years later. (Doolan 1996) Even though this is a proven fake, Piltdown Man is still found in textbooks. Java Man was made from an ape skull and a human femur. Eugene DuBois admitted on his death bed that he had also found a completely human skull at the same level, but he ignored it. He then dismissed Java Man as unrelated parts, but it is still in some textbooks. Lucy, one of our supposed ancestors, has been carefully studied for twenty years and has been determined to be a chimpanzee, a male chimpanzee. Even Donald Johanson admitted that he found the chimp skeleton in one location and the human knee joint in another location. (Wieland 1994) But Johanson still refers to Java Man as a valid fossil. This is just very bad science. Nebraska Man was nothing more than a pig's tooth, and Neanderthal Man is now recognized as totally human. An article in *Creation ex nihilo* in 1994 contained evidence that a Neanderthal Man was found in chain mail armour. (Wieland 1994) Lucia Yaroch, in the Yearbook of Physical Anthropology, 1996, states the following: "The uniqueness of Neanderthals appears to have been exaggerated." (Yaroch 1996) This confession, although quite understated, is a remarkable admission from an evolutionist.

Evolutionists claim one "proof" we descended from apes is that the DNA of humans and chimps is about 97% the same. But that 3-4% difference adds up to a great deal of information. As my dear husband says, "That 3% must be important!" Take a look at the following two sentences that are 97% similar but totally opposite in meanings.

"There are many scientists today who question the evolutionary paradigm and its atheistic, philosophical implications."

"There are not many scientists today who question the evolutionary paradigm with its atheistic, philosophical implications." (Batten 1997)

The following quote is from the same article by Don Batten: "The amount of information in the three million base pairs in the DNA in every human cell has been estimated to be equivalent to that in 1,000 books of 500 pages. If humans were only four percent different this still amounts to 120 million base pairs, equivalent to approximately 12 million words, or 40 large books of information. This is surely an impossible barrier for mutation (random chance) to cross." (Batten 1997)

The fossil record shows remarkable stability of the different species over time. In fact the stability of the species led to a classification system being developed by Carolus Linnaeus (1701-1778). A species is a stable group of plants or animals that usually cannot interbreed with other species. They are "reproductively isolated". (Morris 1974) Being a strong believer in the special creation of Biblical "kinds" in Genesis, Linnaeus sorted and classified the kinds into species. There is a wide variety of possible variations within each species. All dogs, from the tiniest Chihuahua to the largest Great Dane, are all one species,and they are all capable of interbreeding. It is generally accepted that all dogs originated from one type. This is an example of the variation within a species and not the evolution of the DNA molecule from one type to another. This variation is common in most species and only requires a few generations to achieve, not millions of years. (See genetics under the Reproduction Section.) The laws of heredity were developed by Gregor Johann Mendel. Evolution by the mutation of DNA could never have occurred because all mutations that occur are harmful or deadly to the organism. Even given the vast amounts of time required by evolution, there would never be enough beneficial mutations to account for life. Mendel discovered that there was a regular way in which traits were inherited, and his Mendelian Laws became the basis for modern genetics.

Large evolutionary change that would totally alter a species has never been observed. No one has ever seen any transitional fossils. Those fossils that were supposed to be transitional were later proven to be a different species or a deliberate fake. "Natural Selection", which is supposed to be how evolution works, would actually favor a certain species or kind to stay the same. Stable kinds, as seen in the fossil record, would remain stable, while the mutations or the less fit would not reproduce. All we observe in nature is stability or extinction of the species. We see no animals transitioning into a new species. If evolution were true, there would be no stable species at all, but rather everything would be in some form of change into something else. The genetic process that keeps the species stable is powerful evidence that evolution is false.

Have we ever seen an amoebae turning into a fish, or a fish turning into a bird, or a frog turning into a man? Of course not. In literature when a frog turns into a man, it is called a fairy tale. But when a frog turns into a man over a billion years, it is called evolution. Evolutionists think that because they observe homology, similarities in structures of various creatures, that this similarity means the creatures had a common ancestor. To a Creationist, the similarities in different species means that there was one Designer. It is logical that God would use similar structures for similar uses, such as eyes, lungs, bones, hearts, etc. Therefore, similarities in structure, or homology, does not mean a common ancestor but rather that there was one Creator. All things were created by God according to their kind, and they will reproduce only that kind. (Morris 1974)

Scientists in the Middle Ages who were not familiar with the Bible had some very strange ideas about life. It used to be a scientific fact that frogs were spontaneously generated from ponds. It was widely accepted by most townspeople that their pile of garbage generated rats and flies. They observed that there would be no flies or rats in a certain spot until they began to pile their garbage at the edge of town. Then the flies and rats would appear. This made sense to these people. What scientists believe is truth is always changing, and it will always be changing unless it is based in the Word of God that is never changing.

During this time, a fellow named Francesco Redi observed that maggots grew out of spoiled meat (they must have had a lot of spoiled meat back then). So he did an experiment where he put meat into two jars, one covered and one open. Both pieces of meat spoiled, but the meat in the open jar "grew" maggots. Then he noticed that flies landed on the exposed meat and laid eggs and that the maggots actually came from the flies and not the meat. This was not generally accepted, however, until Louis Pasteur boiled some chicken broth in a special glass bottle with an S-curved neck called a swan neck flask. Nothing in the air was allowed to blow into the broth after it was sterilized and no new growth ever occurred. Pasteur concluded that germs in the air blew into exposed broth and that's where the mold came from. In fact this same experiment is on display in a museum in France and shows no growth in over 150 years. Pasteur came up with the Law of Biogenesis that states that "Life always comes from life". This is a <u>scientific law</u> and not a theory. This is provable and repeatable and shows how only life can beget life. (Bliss 1988)

Several scientists have tried to create "life" in a laboratory. Stanley Miller set up an experiment that produced amino acids. The media latched onto this story and announced that he had produced life. He had electrodes discharge a spark into a gaseous mixture of methane (CH_4), ammonia (NH_3) hydrogen (H), and water vapor (H_2O). In order to collect anything out of this heated mixture, Miller knew he had to have a *cold trap* for the products to collect; otherwise, the heat would destroy them faster than they could be produced. It would be extremely difficult to imagine such a cold trap occurring in nature. He did get amino acids but no proteins, and there definitely was some intelligence behind this process, [if you consider the scientist to be intelligent]. This was not random chance. The brown goo that was produced was not life because it contained a 50-50 mixture of right-handed and left-handed amino acids. An explanation of handedness follows in the next paragraph. Amino acids and sugars and other biological molecules, if left to themselves, will tend to cancel each other out and never produce any codes due to the fact that they are half right-handed and half left-handed. Scientists know this and have a serious problem of explaining how these biological molecules could have come together in a "primordial soup" to create life. (Bliss 1988)

Proteins are made of amino acids. Most tissues are made of protein; hair, skin, muscles, etc. But, (and this is a big "but") for life to be possible, all the amino acids in a protein must be LEFT-HANDED. "Handedness" comes from the chemical structure of the amino acids. They are mirror images of each other. A complicated definition is that a left-handed molecule will rotate a plain of polarized light to the left, and a right-handed molecule will rotate a plain of polarized light to the right. The important thing to remember is that these molecules have handedness. The amino acids produced in Miller's experiment were a 50-50 mixture of left-handed and right-handed; therefore, no life would be possible. If even one right-handed molecule would get into an enzyme chain, the whole thing would be useless. This whole process is doubly complicated by the fact that the sugars used by organisms must be 100% right-handed. If only one left-handed sugar occurs in a chain, it would be totally useless. The energy would not be able to be used by the amino acid chain. All living organisms need amino acids and sugars from the very beginning, and all the enzymes and sugars must fit together perfectly. (Wieland 1992)

Proteins are made by DNA; DNA is made up of nucleotides that code for protein. Evolutionists have a real problem with this as to which came first. Creationists have no problem with which came first because God created both simultaneously and fully functional. DNA is a codon molecule that is the blueprint for the correct codes for all the amino acids that make up proteins. DNA is composed of four basic building blocks: guanine, cytosine, adenine, and thymine. These bases, (G,C,A,T) taken three at a time, are called a codon and code for a specific amino acid. Now, the possible combinations of human DNA are 10 to the 87th power. The number of seconds in 4.5 billion years is 10 to the 25th power. That means that if one possible combination of DNA was tried every second for 4.5 billion years by random chance, less than one/third of all the possible combinations could have been tried since (the evolutionists say) the earth began. Random chance would have to get very lucky to get the right combination for human life. It would be as if there were a raffle where 87 tickets were sold ,and you bought 25 tickets, and you were told you were guaranteed to win. Chances are against you. [That is why the gambling establishments are so successful. They know that in games of random chance, you are going to lose].

The man who discovered DNA, Sir Francis Crick, was a strong atheist who totally believed evolution. However, after studying DNA for many years and working with a Pulitzer Prize-winning mathematician on statistical probabilities, he concluded that DNA could not possibly have evolved. Nor could anything ever have evolved. The statistical probability that random chance could have produced anything as complicated as human DNA is equal to the probability that 50 million blind men could all solve the Rubik's Cube at the same time. This is not very likely. Sir Francis Crick has not become a Christian, but he no longer believes in evolution, because he has seen the miracles of the design of DNA.

Evolutionists come up with some very strange arguments to try to prove their point. On a program called "Ultra Science" on The Learning Channel, a group of scientists were talking about changes in the human body and a few individuals' DNA as evidences of evolution occurring. They used Sumo wrestlers in Japan as evidence of evolution occurring today. A Sumo wrestler's DNA has not been altered to create a man of great bulk and strength for fighting. Boys are trained and conditioned from a young age to learn to fight and to eat great quantities of food to build up their size. This is conditioning or adaptation, not a change in the boys' DNA. Another example used was a woman who had conditioned herself to swim in cold water. After fifteen years of swimming in cold water, sleeping with windows open in winter and wearing very light clothes, she developed a layer of fat under her skin, like the Eskimos have, that acted as insulation against the cold and allowed her to swim the English Channel and the Bering Strait. (*Ultra Science* 1995) This, too, is an adaptation. She deliberately conditioned her body to adapt to the cold. Her DNA had not changed. Her children would not be born with an extra layer of fat under their skin, just as the children of Sumo wrestlers would not have large babies. This is not an example of evolution occurring; rather, this is Lamarckism. This is as ludicrous as saying that if a man lost his right arm in an accident, that his children would be born without their right arms. Adaptations are not genetic and are not passed on to the next generation.

Another program of Ultra Science was an interview with geneticist Rebecca Cann who discovered that every race has the same Mitochondrial DNA. Mitochondrial DNA is passed on only from mother to daughter. Dr. Cann's research showed that there were essentially no differences between the races, which led to the conclusion that all humans were related to some original woman. Then she quickly stated that she did not mean to imply that it was a Biblical Adam and Eve, but rather just from a very small population of people. (*Ultra Science* 1995) Even with the evidence staring her right in the face, this intelligent scientist refused to believe what was in front of her, but rather denied the truth of the original Eve, exchanging it for the lie of "a small population of people".

One last interesting fact about DNA is that it has been shown that the DNA of a critter begins to break down, that is it rots, as soon as the critter dies. This degeneration will take about 10,000 years. This means that after 10,000 years there would be no viable DNA left in the organism. Therefore there would be no DNA in anything millions of years old; not in insects trapped in amber, or plant leaves, etc. If any viable DNA was found, say in a bug trapped in amber, it would mean that the critter had to be less than 10,000 years old. This is another enigma for evolutionists but makes perfect sense to a Creationist. (Wieland 1994)

There are groups of scientists around the world and in this country who are spending vast amounts of money looking for signs of intelligent life in outer space. They are trying to determine if a pattern exists in radio signals coming from distant stars, which they would interpret as intelligent life. If these same scientists would just look inside their own bodies, they would find a sign of Supremely Intelligent Life in the very complex pattern and coding of the DNA molecule that is in every one of us created beings.

But consider for a moment, what is the difference between the lifeless moon and the life-filled earth? The answer is WATER. Our planet is over 70% water. It is water that gives our planet its dazzling diversity of life. Water was designed with the properties expressly needed for life.

We are totally dependent on this remarkable substance for life. Water, H_2O, is made of hydrogen and oxygen. Hydrogen gas is the lightest element and is very flammable. Oxygen is the gas that is needed to burn for fire. But when these two gases combine in the proper proportions, the result is water that is used to fight fire!

Water is H_2O in the liquid state. It becomes a solid at 32° Fahrenheit and a gas at 212° Fahrenheit. One ounce of water contains a trillion, trillion molecules. What makes water so amazing and powerful is its configuration. It looks like Mickey Mouse ears. The large oxygen ion with a -2 valence has two smaller hydrogen ions with a valence of +1 each that are bonded to it at an angle of 105°. This makes water a dipolar molecule (positive on one end and negative on the other) and affords it its unique properties. The atoms of hydrogen and oxygen are quick to join and difficult to separate. The dipolar molecule is a remarkable solvent, and given enough time will dissolve almost any other substance.

In the solid state, most other substances will become more dense than their liquid and sink. This is because they shrink as the temperature drops. But water is different. It will shrink until about 40 degrees; then it starts to expand and become less dense until it expands by 9% in volume when solid. This is why ice floats in water. The fact that ice floats is critical to life on earth. Floating ice on the surface of a lake protects the water beneath from further freezing. If ice became heavier and sank to the bottom, all rivers, lakes and seas would freeze solid. There would be no chance for life to survive. But God designed water differently. Ice floats and then melts when the temperature rises. Rain water washes the air for us removing the carbon dioxide and returning it to the plants that use it. This is not a random chance molecule. This was designed for us by our Creator. (*Dust or Destiny*)

The Bible says "All the rivers run into the sea; yet the sea is not full; unto the place from whence the rivers come, thither they return again." (Eccl. 1:7 KJV) This describes the water cycle. More energy is expended in the water cycle in one day than man has generated in all of history.

We need water for our physical life, and the formula for it cannot be changed. Jesus is the Living Water, and we need Him for our spiritual life; the formula for that cannot be changed. We would die without water; our spirits would die without the Living Water. The formula for both is simple but very exact, and there is only one way. The Living Water is yours for free, but you must receive it to live. Revelation 22:17 says, "Whoever is thirsty, let him come; and whoever wishes, let him take the free gift of the water of life."

IX. THE SENSES

Consider the incredible gift of our senses. If one has never been blind or deaf, it is hard to imagine life without these senses. Some people have a disease that causes them not to be able to feel pain or any sensation. People who have lost the sense of sight find that they have heightened senses of smell and touch far beyond that of a sighted person. Our senses help us to enjoy and appreciate the beautiful creation God has given to us. As we begin to understand the marvelous design and the incredible sensitivity of our senses, we can more fully understand what God has done for us.

The biomechanics of hearing, which involve the complexities of transferring sound wave energy into mechanical energy and then into electrical energy as impulses to the brain that are received as hearing, are enormously involved. Scientists do not fully understand how we hear or see. The sound produced is actually replayed on another instrument inside the ear. The part of the ear that you see directs sound into the ear canal. Sound is really invisible vibration (waves) in the air. Vibrations move the eardrum or **tympanic membrane** which is attached to the three tiniest bones in the human body, the bones of the middle ear (hammer, anvil, stirrup), causing them to move. These bones are fully developed at birth and are the same size in a baby and an adult. Why? Is this just an accident? The motion of these bones cause motion in the fluid in the **cochlea** which is a fluid-filled spiral. Waves in this fluid, the **perilymph fluid**, move against a membrane to which are attached the hair cells, 16,000 in each ear. These sound receptors are under constant siege from the cumulative effects of age, drugs and loud noise. Yet, the 32,000 **hair cells** are all that stand between hearing and silence. On top of each hair cell are even tinier hairs called **stereocilia**. The stereocilia brush against the tectorial membrane which changes the motion into electrical impulses. Auditory nerve impulses from the cochlea travel along the cochlear nerve and through the pons to the brain's auditory cortex. These nerve impulses are then sent to the brain, our brain tells us when we have just heard something. All this happens instantaneously! Not only that, but since we have ears on both sides of our head about six inches apart, sound waves from a source reach each ear at slightly different times. Then our super computer, our brain, calculates the different arrival times, interprets them and gives us an idea as to where the sound came from. (Discover 1993)

This system is elaborate, sensitive and ingenious. I know I would have not designed a hearing system this way; it sounds like a Rube Goldberg device to me. But God, in His infinite wisdom and creativity, designed this hearing system for us. Not only do we hear, but the perilymph fluid in the cochlea helps us maintain our balance. Nothing that intricate and complicated could have happened by chance. Remember that faith comes by hearing the Word of God.

A look at how we see can be very revealing. Our eyes carry information about what we are looking at, but it is the brain that actually "sees". The receptors in our eyes are only part of the process of vision. The brain has to weave together many bits of information about motion, form, depth and color for us to see. The iris is the colored part of the eye. The pupil enlarges or decreases in size to allow the proper amount of light into the eye. Light passes through the lens and the clear jelly inside the eyeball and is inverted on the retina at the back of the eye. The lens of the eye has an auto-focus of strong muscles that change the focus rapidly depending on what we are looking at. The retina at the back of the eye contains the rods and cones that send messages along the optic nerve to the brain. The pieces of the picture are interpreted by a complex network of processing centers. (Gray 1977) Even when the sense of sight has been lost, the brain can compensate by enhancing the other senses. A program called "Body Works" on The Learning Channel showed a blind man who could create beautiful portraits of his subjects just by feeling them with his hands. His brain allowed him to "see" through his hands. (*Body Works* 1995)

We see beautiful colors and pictures that are not still but in motion. God gave us movies with Technicolor and sound! The brain takes signals from the retinas and relays them through the lateral geniculate bodies, and then passes them to areas in the back of the brain. Other areas of the brain are involved which are yet unidentified. (Gray 1977) Where the optic nerve attaches to the retina, there is a blind spot fifteen degrees off center. Yet, as we look around there is no black hole in our visual field because the brain fills it in for us. Even Darwin himself said, "To suppose that the eye could have been formed by natural selection seems absurd in the highest degree." These amazing organs of sight that God has given us allow us to view His creation. The colors we see also have meaning as expressed in the Bible. Blue was used on the priests' garments and in the temple to remind the people of Heaven and their heavenly character. Purple was the color of royalty. Red represents the Blood of Jesus, but crimson and scarlet were used to represent sin. Green is the color of praise. Judah, whose name means praise, wrote his name on the emerald on the breast plate of the High Priest. White, of course, means purity and sinlessness. I was curious about how the Blood of Jesus could make us whiter than the snow. Snow seems to be very white. However, [I just learned recently that] inside every snowflake is a microscopic speck of dust around which the ice will crystallize. When the Blood of Jesus Christ makes us whiter than the snow, you can believe it totally. Jesus will remove even the smallest speck of sin from our lives.

Our eyes are windows to the soul. We can tell by looking at someone if he is happy ,sad, mean, joyful, someone we should stay away from, or someone who needs comforting. As Christians we should always project an image of Jesus and His lifestyle because as the song says, "You're the only Jesus some people will ever see".

Smell and taste are chemical senses. The chemical receptors on our tongue sense four basic things - sweet, sour, salty, and bitter - but provide us an incredible variety of flavors, from chocolate, strawberries and ice cream, to castor oil and lemons. The sense of taste tells us whether a certain item is to be enjoyed or avoided. Taste is actually a combination of taste and smell. Anyone who has ever had a stuffy head knows that the nose enhances the ability to taste. Molecules of food (chocolate) are drawn up into the olfactory neurons as air is inhaled through the nose.These neurons have cilia on the ends, covered in mucous, that carry the receptors for odor molecules. (Smith 1989 and A.D.A.M. 1996) When these molecules bind with the receptors, the neurons send messages to the olfactory bulbs and to various parts of the brain for interpretation. While the **olfactory neurons** are doing their job, some molecules of food (chocolate) pass over taste buds on the tongue, which sit in little wells. Neurons associated with these taste cells relay their messages about taste to the brain. But not just about taste, the tongue also sends signals about texture (creamy or coarse and rough) and temperature (hot or cold). Only liquids can get into the taste buds, so we have saliva in our mouths. Chewing breaks down food into pieces and saliva carries it to the taste cells. (*Discover* 1993) Think of all the wonderful things that we like to eat and how they taste. God has given us many good things to eat for the nourishment and health of our bodies. God also tells us to "Taste and see that the Lord is good." (Ps. 34:8) We are to take in God's Word daily for the health of our spirits.

Touching is an important sense. We are people who love to touch. We hug and shake hands and pat dogs and touch nice, soft things. I couldn't make it through the day without hugs from my boys and my husband. Touch involves very complex neural circuitry. Nerve signals from all over the body are sent to the thalamus, a little organ in the middle of the brain. This structure has sections made up of neurons that are assigned to every area of the body. From this central structure, signals are sent on to neurons in the **somatosensory cortex**, which contains the brain's map of the body. This representation of the body would look a little strange to us because since the hands and lips and face contain the most receptors, they have a large area in the cortex. Arms and legs would have much smaller areas. Hands would be the largest since they have the most neurons. People who have lost limbs may still experience the sensation of "feeling" in a missing hand or leg. Even though the limb is gone, the neurons in the somatosensory cortex are still there. This sensation is known as *phantom limbs*. (*Discover Magazine* 1993) This complex circuitry allows us the sensory range from touching soft baby skin to having a thumb smashed with a hammer. This is more than just touch sensations because when there is tissue damage, a whole other system goes into action to repair the damage. Gentle touching is enjoyable, and hard touching can be painful. When we reach out to touch other people's lives for Jesus, we must do it in a gentle way that will be appealing to them and not a hard or harsh way that might cause them to move away from the things of the Lord.

X. LANGUAGE

One of the most interesting things about humans is that they have a spoken language. Even the most so-called 'primitive' cultures have a spoken language. Language gives humans an advantage over animals in communication and learning and writing. Yes, chimpanzees can learn and respond to some commands and can even communicate in a limited sign language. But animals in the wild respond to signs and sounds from their fellow critters. Just because chimps can understand and respond to certain sounds does not mean that they understand language. Many pets can do the same thing. Dogs, cats, parakeets, rats, and other pets very definitely respond to commands and to love. But it doesn't mean that they understand grammar or sentence structure. I can say to my dog, "You're so sweet and cute." But if I use a harsh tone in my voice he will respond as if I had scolded him. On the other hand, if I say, "You bad puppy, why did you make that mess!" in a sweet tone of voice, he will probably wag his tail and lick me. They get more cues from the way you say something rather than what you say, because they don't understand words.

No ape or any other animal can write a sentence, no matter how many researchers say their charges have special intelligence. They cannot conjugate verbs or have any concept of what a book is. A program on the Discovery Channel called "Animal Intelligence" was arguing this point. Some scientists were convinced that their animals understood words. Other scientists said that the animals merely were responding to slight variation in the researcher's posture or facial expressions. (*Animal Intelligence* 1995)

Animals react on instinct. Instinct is a very important quality that God has given to animals for their survival. But they have no ability to conceive of, or to understand, abstract ideas. They communicate with vocalizations that indicate an emergency situation, hunger, a desire to mate, etc. There is no difference in the way a dog barks in Dallas or in Peking. They don't bark in Chinese or Russian. But they can understand the sounds for certain responses in the language of their owners. Dogs are very intelligent and so are apes, but they have no way of knowing what the symbols on this page stand for. Dogs and apes respond to human affection, and I believe that is why some researchers personify the apes' behavior, giving them human characteristics that really are not there. Some animals have the ability to mimic human speech and sounds but can never put words together in new ways to make sense. (Pitman 1984) The letters BAT convey meaning: either a stick to hit a small sphere or a flying mammal. However, BAT means something entirely different in Japanese, Spanish or Hebrew. So, our brains must not only recognize certain groups of letters but also associate meaning with those groups.

For example, when my youngest son was learning to talk, we were teaching him various words out of a Richard Scarry book about jobs. A painter is a man who paints. A builder is a man who builds. A driver is a man who drives. So, one day he saw the mailman coming with mail for us and said, "Mom, here comes the mailer." That was incorrect, but what an incredible leap of logic! He was never taught to say "mailer", but to him the man who brings the mail must be the "mailer". No animal could ever make a conclusion about a word in this manner.

Why would we even need to evolve language? If other animals get along just fine with a few sounds and gestures, why couldn't we? Deaf people communicate rather well with hand gestures. Why didn't we just develop sign language? The answer is we didn't evolve. God created us this way to be able to communicate and understand each other and Himself, better. No animal, dog, cat, ape, whatever, has any concept of God as a Divine Being. Language and literacy are gifts from God.

I recently enjoyed a program on The Learning Channel called *Body Works* that was evaluating human communication. Humans are very good at using their faces and hands for communication. Faces can be read; hands show emotion; and only humans say "good-bye". When I heard that remark I paid closer attention because I thought it was very interesting. Animals will greet one another, but only humans say "good-bye". The human face has seventy-four muscles that are capable of making 7000 expressions that are recognized by other people. Only humans have handshakes, ceremonies, burials, weddings, celebrations, a concept of God and spirit, and abstract ideas. Only humans have creativity such as is expressed in art, music, poems, inventions, literature, etc. Creativity is exclusively human. (Body Works 1995)

If humans can communicate so well with our faces and hands, why would we need to "evolve" speech ? Why would we ever "evolve" handshakes or ceremonies? These things are not necessary to the lives of dogs or apes. Only things that are necessary and beneficial are passed on to the next generation in evolution. They would never have evolved.

One of the most astonishing things that the brain does for us is to compensate for a lost ability, such as when a blind person can "see" with his hands. This program, *Body Works*, showed a man who was blinded by a grenade in Vietnam at the age of twenty-three. He is now forty-three and creates beautiful sculptures of people. He feels the people with his hands, next he feels the surface of his marble or wood, and then he sculpts incredible figures. His brain has allowed his hands to compensate for his lost vision. To his brain, he "sees" through his hands. (*Body Works* 1995)

Only God could build in such an ability for the body and brain to compensate like this. In the wild, when an animal loses its ability to see or smell or hunt, it usually dies. There is no compensation for the loss of other senses. This is not an ability that would have evolved, because all the disabled animals would have died.

XI. RACES

All human beings alive today are descendants of Noah and his family, the eight people who survived the Flood on the ark. It is possible to show through genetics that all skin colors can be generated from two people of medium skin color, containing the dominant genes for dark skin and the recessive genes for light skin. The only skin coloring anyone has is the pigment melanin. Some people have more, some people have less, but it's all the same pigment. People with dark skin have larger amounts of melanin. People who have light skin have lower amounts of melanin. Orientals who have yellow skin have a layer of fat just underneath the skin that gives it a yellowish color. American Indians whose skin is redder have many small capillaries under the skin. My husband and I have three boys with three different skin tones.

A Professor of Genetics at the University of California, Francisco Ayala, has calculated that an average human couple would have to have 10 to the 2017th power children before they would have one child identical to another. That's a lot of kids, and a lot of variability. And most scientists believe that there are only 10 to the 80th power atoms in all the visible universe. (Pitman 1984)

The different amounts of this pigment a person inherits depends on two pairs of genes. A child will inherit half of each pair from each parent. (See genetics in section on Reproduction.) It can be shown through genetics that all races could have developed from Noah and his family in just a few generations. An analysis of the distribution of people after the confounding of language at the Tower of Babel indicated that the descendants of Ham went south into the area that is now Egypt. The descendants of Japheth went north into the area of Europe. And that the descendants of Shem went into the area of the Middle East. (Stanton and Hyma 1992)

I don't know how He did it, but God could have given the people with similar skin color the same language at the Tower of Babel. People who could understand each other would then get together and probably stay together. Since the genes would be more similar and mixing of the genes would occur less and less, then either the dominant or recessive characteristics would be retained in that population group.

XII. HUMAN HISTORY

Population statistics provide one of the strongest evidences for recent creation. World population has grown only slowly in the past. During the time of Christ the entire population was less than 500 million or half a billion. In 1659 world population was 545 million and then increased more rapidly to 2.5 billion by 1950. It had reached 4.5 billion by 1985 and is expected to be 6 billion by the year 2000. (Baker 1976) The present rate of growth for the population is 2% per year. But at this rate it would only take 1100 years to reach a population of 3.5 billion people on the planet. If we assume a growth of 1/2% then it would take 4500 years to reach 5 billion. This fits in very well with the event of Noah's Flood and his family repopulating the world. Evolutionists tell us that man has been around for about 3 million years. But even if we are very conservative and use the 1/2% growth rate, that would mean that the number of people who have been born and have died would be 10 to the 2155th power. That is a staggering amount of people when you consider that there are probably only 10 to the 80th power atoms in the entire universe. (Morris 1974) This would mean that there would be dozens of graves on every acre of our planet. However, ancient human bones are extremely rare. They are not found because there has never been a million years of human generations.

The earth isn't even full now with five billion people on it. One study of the population concluded that the entire population of the world could fit in the state of Texas allowing 1200 square feet for each person. (Human Life International) So we are a long way from filling up the earth now. But, if given a million years, it would be pretty crowded.

Man was created in the image of God; therefore, ancient man was not ignorant. Some of us who live in the last half of the 20th century think that we are the only people who have ever occupied the Earth that have ever invented clever machines or displayed amazing feats of technology and engineering. Ancient men were brilliant artists and problem-solvers. Adam was given the task of naming all the animals, so he was no dummy.

Some scientists give "ancient astronauts" the credit for the wonders of the ancient world. But that theory just extends the question of creation, because who would have created the ancient astronauts? Man does not need any outside help; even God said at the Tower of Babel that there was nothing they could not do. Those ancient people were not less intelligent than people today. There is no evidence that the human brain has evolved at all during the last 50,000 years. Evolution sees the history of man as a steady progress through time, and that dismisses any accomplishments of older civilizations.

Medieval Baghdad had an efficient postal service, banks, and a paper mill. France has had calendars for many thousands of years. American Indians had high-rise apartment condos. Ancient Greeks used an early form of computer and discovered the steam engine. Physicians in India performed plastic surgery in 1 B.C. Turkey had very sophisticated city structures 4000 - 5000 years ago. They were complete with regular streets, and brick homes around courtyards; interior walls were plastered and painted with murals. The people of ancient Turkey were very intelligent; they excelled in agriculture, farming, and raising cattle. They made pottery, metal tools, woven linen clothing, made mirrors and fancy jewelry. (James and Thorpe 1994)

Alexander the Great submerged himself in the world's first diving bell. One of his cities, Alexandria, in Egypt, was a large metropolis of 500,000 people in 200 B.C. They built the world's first lighthouse that could be seen for hundreds of miles. They had a university with a library of half a million volumes. They performed in theaters with mechanical figures and moving scenery. They had buildings with automatic sliding doors, slot machines, luxury liners with multiple decks and steam engines. Clearly these people were not less intelligent. (*Seven Wonders* 1995)

The Romans, before Christ, engineered an amazing aqueduct and plumbing system, roads that still exist today, an elaborate defense system, apartment buildings and lighthouses. The system of highways and roads that the Romans built was already in place by the time the disciples of Jesus went out to spread the Gospel. And because the roads were there, they were able to travel farther and easier than they would have otherwise. The Romans also built great harbors, such as the one built by King Herod from 22 B.C. to 9 B.C. that was bigger than the one in Athens, had an artificial breakwater, was 200 feet wide, and had a city on its walls. Most historians thought that the record of this harbor was just the boastful writings of the Jewish historian, Josephus, until 1960 when discoveries proved it to be true. The co-director of the Ceasarea excavation, Dr. Avner Raban had this to say, "This Herodian port is an example of a 21st century harbor built 2,000 years ago. In fact, if the modern harbors of Ashdod and Haifa had employed such systems of design and engineering, they would not have had the problems they face today." (James and Thorpe 1994)

While Europe was in the "dark ages", Arabs thrived in an advanced civilization with an enormous free hospital with 1000 physicians, a postal service, numerous banks with branches in other countries, a water supply and irrigation system, a sewage system, and a paper mill. At the same time the Ancient Aztecs built a city with a huge marketplace, drugstores, canals with portable bridges, ball game courts, a floating garden, enormous zoos and floral collections. When the Spanish invaders first saw it, they thought they were dreaming. (James and Thorpe 1994)

Calendars and writings have been around as long as there have been people on the earth. Adam and his descendants kept written genealogies of everyone who was born. The Old Testament patriarchs were gifted by God with all sorts of talents from farming to music to metal work. Man did not start out unintelligent and gradually become smart over the centuries. Man was created with intelligence and creativity.

After Noah's flood, some people did live in caves and have what we would call "a primitive life", but there are people all over the world alive today who live "a primitive life". That life style does not exist only in antiquity, but is also contemporary. The Amish people choose to live without electricity and other modern conveniences but it does not mean they are less intelligent; they are very clever and resourceful. An Australian Aborigine who was dressed in a three-piece suit and raised on Wall Street would function perfectly well in that environment. But the evolutionist would like us to think that ancient man was more like an animal and therefore had to evolve to our present state of intelligence. God created man as man, not ape-man, and the first man was very intelligent.

The ancient astronomers very carefully charted the movements of the stars and planets and were able to accurately predict their movements and even eclipses of the sun and moon. The ancient Egyptians built pyramids and temples that accurately line up with certain constellations. It is a scientific arrogance of today that says these people needed outside assistance from "ancient astronauts" to accomplish these great things. Ancient man was just as intelligent as man today, if not more so. There have been many accomplishments of the past that we do not have the technology to reproduce, such as the huge monoliths that were used to build the pyramids and the temples. Some ancient civilizations created the huge carvings on Easter Island and the structure at Stonehenge that modern scientists cannot explain. Even God said at the Tower of Babel in Genesis 11:6, "If as one people speaking the same language they have begun to do this, then nothing they plan to do will be impossible for them."

The following is a partial list of the contributions of Christian men who were outstanding in their field of science, taken from the book *Men of Science/ Men of God* by Dr. Henry Morris:

Charles Babbage - Computers and calculators
Francis Bacon - the Scientific Method
Michael Faraday - Electro-magnetics, electric generator, electrical field theory
Johann Kepler - Physical Astronomy, celestial mechanics, ephermeris tables
Matthew Maury - Oceanography, Hydrography
Issac Newton - Calculus, Law of Gravity, reflecting telescope, dynamics
Louis Pasteur - Law of Biogenesis, Pasteurization, vaccinations, fermentation

God created man intelligent from the very beginning. People have always been creative, inventive, and productive. The book of Genesis talks about the descendants of Adam and Eve and all the abilities with which they were endowed. When modern

51

archaeologists discover some ancient civilization with its sophisticated accomplishments, they are amazed at how some primitive culture could have achieved such wonderful things. However, if you look at the prime achievements of many cultures, you will find that most of them occurred in the past. The Greeks, Mayans, and Mesopotamians had their Golden Ages around 500 B.C. The Roman culture was at its peak at the time of Christ. The Pharaohs of Egypt ruled 1500 B.C. The city of Ur where Abraham lived was a huge metropolis 4000 years ago. (Petersen 1986)

There are scientists today who are contributing to our knowledge of Creation Science: Dr.Henry Morris and Dr. John Morris of the Institute for Creation Research; Steve Austin, a geologist who has studied Mt. St. Helens and the Grand Canyon as evidence for the Flood; Robert Gentry, whose work in the field of radiometric dating has uncovered evidence that the earth had to have formed suddenly. There are physicists and paleontologists and hundreds of scientists who are in the ranks of Creation Scientists. These men and women base their science on the Word of God. We must not fall into the trap of believing everything a person says just because that person is a scientist. The fascinating "new discovery" that makes it to the 6:00 news is usually critically debated and dismantled in the scientific journals. But the report of how the latest and greatest discovery fizzled out under close scrutiny never makes it to the 6:00 news. What scientists believe as the truth is always changing and will always change unless it is based on the Bible. We must study to show ourselves approved of God. "Do your best to present yourself to God as one approved, a workman who does not need to be ashamed and who correctly handles the word of truth. Avoid godless chatter, because those who indulge in it will become more and more ungodly." (2 Timothy 2:15-16)

~ Jill Whitlock

SECTION 2: GRADES K-12

TEACHING FORMAT INSTRUCTIONS

TEXT OUTLINE

SAMPLE LESSON PLANS

READING LIST

ACTIVITY/EXPERIMENT RESOURCE LIST

VOCABULARY/SPELLING LIST

VOCABULARY/SPELLING/LANGUAGE ARTS SUGGESTIONS

MATH REINFORCEMENT

SCIENCE ACTIVITIES/EXPERIMENTS

GEOGRAPHY/HISTORY REINFORCEMENT

ART/MUSIC REINFORCEMENT

Creation Anatomy Outline
Grades K-3

I. The Price of the Human Body

A. Scripture: 1 Corinthians 12:12-27

B. Value of Materials

C. Price Paid

II. Blood, Heart and Lungs

A. Scripture: Leviticus 17:4

B. Definition and Function

C. Facts

D. Heart as a Muscle

E. Parts of the Blood

F. Lungs and Breathing

III. Injuries and Healing

A. Blood Cells

    1. Red Cells

    2. White Cells

    3. Platelets (Blood clotting)

B. Immunization (Shots)

    1. Lymph System

    2. Germs

    3. "New" Science

IV. Bones & Muscles

A. Framework

B. Muscles

    1. How they work

    2. Types

C. Joints

D. Hands

V. Digestive System

A. Mouth

B. Teeth

C. Saliva

D. Esophagus

E. Stomach

F. Liver

G. Small Intestines

H. Large Intestines

I. Kidneys

VI. Nervous System and Brain

VII. Senses

A. Eyes (Sight)

B. Ears (Hearing)

C. Mouth (Taste)

D. Nose (Smell)

E. Skin (Touch)

VIII. Language

IX. Races

X. Human History

A. Achievement

B. Invention

C. Population

Lesson Plans

Subject Date:	Monday	Tuesday	Wednesday	Thursday	Friday
Bible/Religion Studies					
Teaching Outline					
Reading Section					
Language Arts/Spelling/ Vocabulary					
Math Reinforcement					
Science Activities and Experiments					
Geography/History					
Art/Music					

CR= Creation Resource   TS= Teacher Selection

Lesson Plans: Grades K-3 Week 1

Bible/ Religion Studies
Monday –Thursday: 1 Cor. 12:12-27 (dictation / memory work) ; **Friday:** Lev. 17:14; Gen 2: 7; teacher's selection of additional verses/lessons

Teaching Outline
Monday: I a,b,c II-a,b; **Tuesday:** review II-,c,d ; **Wednesday**: II e,f ; **Thursday:** II e,f continued; **Friday: review;** II a,b,c,d,e,f

Language Arts/Math/History/Music/Art
Monday: assign vocabulary words, write definitions on index cards; write each word five times; read sections in Teaching Outline on price of human body (Lev. 17:14); use resource books for information on circulatory system; discuss the heart/parts/function of heart; draw/label parts of heart; discuss process of the scientific method and importance in using process when studying science; locate pulse points in wrist/neck; using pulse rate hand-out, record heart/pulse rate;

Tuesday: use vocabulary words in sentence/write words five times each; squeeze tennis ball (activity); make pulse meter; continue to record pulse/heart rate;

Wednesday: write vocabulary words five times each; make stethoscope; listen to heart/beat; sing song about heart; discuss how many miles of blood vessels are in human body; practice mapping/reading skills; make drawing of blood cells; make diagram of lung; record how many breaths taken in a minute/five minutes; discuss chest colds/flem; name parts of the lung; write your words 5 times.

Thursday: write vocabulary words five times each; take a practice spelling test; review definitions; measure chest expansion when inhaling/exhaling; record how long student can hold their breath; place hand mirror in refrigerator for an hour, remove wipe surface and have student breath on it. Discuss what happens to mirror; review parts of heart/lungs and functions of each.

Friday: orally ask definitions of vocabulary; take spelling test if necessary; play the Stepping Hearts game; read about Dr. Christian Barnard and first heart transplant; locate where Dr. Barnard was from; pretend you are in Miss Frizzle's class and add dialogue to the story/act out the scene; sing "There is Power in the Blood" and other songs pertaining to blood.

Lesson Plans Grades K-3 Week 2

Bible/ Religion Studies
Monday—Friday: teacher's choice of verses and lessons

Teaching Outline
Monday-Review **Tuesday**-III-a-1,2,3 **Wednesday**-III-b1,2,3 **Thursday**– Review, **Friday**– reports and presentations

Language Arts/Math/History/Music/Art
Monday: assign vocabulary words/write definitions on index cards, write each five times each; read in Teaching Outline/resource books about blood cells; make life-size drawing of student's body; label organs studied thus far; review by playing the Jumping Bee Game; review respiration using Scientific method; continue recording heart rates after exercise.

Tuesday: use vocabulary words in a sentence, write words five times each; choose a sentence from a resource book for dictation; make drawing of blood cells/review job of each cell; discuss what cells are made of; exercise and record pulse rate; read book about scientist Galen/ask comprehension questions; locate where Galen lived on map; sing "Be Careful Little Eyes What You See" or other body part songs.

Wednesday: write words five times each/alphabetize the words; select the best sentence to copy using the best handwriting/printing; add lymph system to body drawing/read about this system and how it keeps you healthy; study healing process of a scrape/cut; exercise/record pulse rates; discuss germs and how they intrude human body/importance of keeping hands clean; discuss some of the greatest epidemics in history;

Thursday: spell vocabulary words orally; take practice test; make up a chapter for the *Magic School Bus* about what happens in the body when someone scrapes their elbow; review week's content; discuss who discovered penicillin; make a commercial/public service announcement about pros/cons of immunizations/flu shots.

Friday: add the new vocabulary to play the Stepping Heart Game; review definitions and take the spelling test; review week's content; review body drawing/name all parts; perform commercial/PSA; present experiments/reports done during week.

Lesson Plans Grades K-3 Week 3

Bible/ Religion Studies
Monday—Friday: Job 10: 8-11; teacher's choice of verses and lessons

Teaching Outline
Monday: IV-a, b; **Tuesday:** IV-b1, b2: **Wednesday:** IV-c, d; **Thursday:** IV d, review; **Friday:** reports and presentations

Language Arts/Math/Science/History/Music/Art
Monday: assign vocabulary words/write definitions on index cards; write words five times each; record heart/pulse rate after exercise; review skeletal system from resource books; choose experiments/activities for the week; add larger bones to body drawing; sing "Head Bone is Connected to Neck Bone"; get soup bones/ observe marrow; discuss what happens in the marrow of bones.

Tuesday: use vocabulary words in a sentence/write words five times each; review bones; discuss how many bones in human body; discuss major bones/functions of bones; name parts of bone; discuss how to keep bones strong; make drawing of different types of muscles; build model of arm to explore how muscles extend/ contract.

Wednesday: write vocabulary words five times each/alphabetize the words; have older students include words from previous weeks; select the best sentence to copy using the best handwriting/printing; check out Easy Hands on Models that Teach by Donald M. Silver/read section on joints; discuss tendons/ligaments; re-search scientists Luigi Galvani/Alessandro Volta and Sir Humphrey Davy and each contribution to discoveries of the human body/muscles and their work; lo-cate where each scientist lived on map/globe.

Thursday: spell vocabulary words orally/take practice test; play the Stepping Hearts Game with new and old vocabulary; work on picking out nouns and find-ing the subject in your sentences; finish models/experiments for week; do dissec-tion of muscle tissue/examine joints of raw piece of chicken; prepare presenta-tions for Friday.

Friday: give oral spelling/vocabulary test; play Jumping Bee Game to review spelling/definitions of words; continue to write dialogue into the *Magic School Bus* story as if your student is part of that story; present any reports/experiments.

Lesson Plans K-3 Week 4

Bible/ Religion Studies
Monday—Friday: Genesis 1:29-30; additional teacher's choice of verses and lessons

Teaching Outline
Monday: V-a, b, c; **Tuesday:** V-d, e, f; **Wednesday:** V-g, h, I; **Thursday:** review **Friday:** reports/presentations.

Language Arts/Math/Science/History/Music/Art

Monday: assign vocabulary words/write definitions on index cards; write each word five times each; from resource books/outline, read about mouth/tongue/ saliva/teeth; discuss what happens during the chewing process; discuss concept of food as fuel/why eating good food is important; contact dental office for possible field trip/have student compile interviewing questions to ask dentist or hygienist; have student write report on field trip; diagram inside of mouth/locate where saliva glands are located; add teeth to body drawing.

Tuesday: use vocabulary words in a sentence; write words five times each; make up short rhymes using your words; add the esophagus/stomach/liver to your body drawing; check your resource books for experiments to enhance week's lesson;.

Wednesday: write words five times each/alphabetize words; have older students include words from previous weeks; select the best sentence to copy using the best handwriting/printing; add the small intestine/large intestine/kidneys to life-size body drawing; discuss length of intestines; continue working on experiments/ models selected for the week.

Thursday: spell vocabulary words orally; take practice test; play the Stepping Hearts Game with new and old vocabulary; work with picking out nouns and finding the subject in your sentences; learn about verbs; write simple report on one of the organs studied this week; continue working on experiments; search for pictures of organs studied and make a collage.

Friday: play Jumping Bee Game to review spelling and definitions of words, take the spelling test; continue to add dialogue in the *Magic School Bus* story if that is a fun activity for your students; read any reports/show models and experiments using scientific method sheets.

Lesson Plans Grades K-3 Week 5

Bible/ Religion Studies
Monday—Friday: Phil 4: 8, teachers choice of additional verses/lessons.

Teaching Outline
Monday: parts of brain; **Tuesday**: pituitary gland, brainstem (involuntary activities), hypothalamus, thalamus; **Wednesday**: nerves; **Thursday**: review; **Friday**: reports and presentations.

Language Arts/Math/Science/History/Music/Art

Monday: assign vocabulary words/write definitions on index cards; write each word five times each; from resource books, read about the brain; name parts of brain; print off diagram of brain for students and have them label; discuss function/facts of cerebrum/cerebellum; exercise and record heart/pulse rate; discuss part of brain used to answer questions/for memorization.

Tuesday: use vocabulary words in a sentence, write words five times each; begin making cards for the Stepping Hearts Game; discuss pituitary gland/brainstem (involuntary activities), hypothalamus, thalamus; play memory games.

Wednesday: write words five times each/alphabetize the words; have older students include words from previous weeks; write or dictate your Bible verse and rewrite practicing penmanship; discuss spinal cord/nerves as the body's messaging system; discuss how brain/spinal cord injuries occur during car accidents/sports or recreational activities and how these injuries effect people; discuss ways to protect your brain.

Thursday: spell vocabulary words orally, take practice test; play the Stepping Hearts Game with new and old vocabulary; work on picking out nouns, finding the subjects and verbs in your sentences; test your student's memory by giving another blank diagram of the brain and see if your students can name all the parts; choose further experiments from your resource books; make a clay model of brain using different colored clay to show parts of brain.

Friday: play Jumping Bee Game to review spelling and definitions of words, take the spelling test; present any reports/experiments using scientific method.

Lesson Plans Grades K-3 Week 6

Bible/ Religion Studies
Monday—Friday: Ps 33:18, Ps 119: 103, Proverbs 1:8; teachers choice of additional verses/lessons

Teaching Outline
Monday: eyes/ sight; **Tuesday**: ear-hearing; **Wednesday**: tongue-taste; **Thursday**: review; **Friday**: reports/presentations

Language Arts/Math/Science/History/Math/Art

Monday: assign vocabulary words/write definitions on index cards; write words five times each; from resource books, read about eye/sight; name parts of eye; discuss function/facts of the eye; discuss blinking as voluntary/involuntary action; look at eyes in the mirror and name parts you can see; take flash light into darkened room to examine how pupil of eye opens/closes depending on amount of light available; sing "Be Careful Little Eyes"; record heart/pulse rate after exercise.

Tuesday: use vocabulary words in a sentence, write words five times each; begin making cards for the Stepping Hearts Game; discuss ear/hearing; from resource books read about ear and hearing; name parts of eye/ear; discuss functions/facts of ear; make chart of senses; get a book on sign language and review.

Wednesday: write vocabulary words five times each alphabetize the words; have older students include words from previous weeks; write or dictate your Bible verse and rewrite practicing penmanship; discuss the tongue/taste; from resource books read about the sense of taste; label/diagram tongue; experiment with different foods by placing them on the tongue in different places.

Thursday: spell words orally, take practice test; play the Stepping Hearts game with new and old vocabulary; work with picking out nouns and verbs; learn about adjectives; review material learned this week; discuss the role/work of an audiologist; discuss who invented sign language; practice some simple sign language; make survey of family members who use devices to enhance senses (hearing aids, eye glasses, contact lenses, etc); research who invented each device.

Friday: play Jumping Bee Game to review spelling and definitions of words, take the spelling test; present any reports/experiments from the week's lesson.

Lesson Plans Grades K-3 Week 7

Bible/ Religion Studies
Monday—Friday: Phil. 4:18, Mark 5:28, Genesis 11: 1-9; teachers selection of additional verses/lessons.

Teaching Outline
Monday: smell/ nose; **Tuesday**: touch/skin; **Wednesday**: language; **Thursday**: review; **Friday**: reports/presentations.

Language Arts/Math/Science/History/Music/Art

Monday: assign vocabulary words/write definitions on index cards; write each word five times each; from resource books, read about nose/smell; name parts of nose; discuss function/facts of nose; blind-fold students to see how well they can name items placed under nose (orange, cinnamon, peanut butter, etc.); discuss how sense of smell and taste are connected; continue recording heart/pulse rate; add eyes/ear/mouth to body drawing.

Tuesday: use vocabulary words in a sentence; write words five times each; begin making cards for the Stepping Hearts Game; read about skin/sense of touch; discuss skin as largest organ of the body; discuss how skin protects/regulates body temperature; print out skin diagram and have students label parts; study fingerprints; do thumb print art; choose experiments for the week.

Wednesday: write vocabulary words five times each and alphabetize the words; have older students include words from previous weeks; write or dictate your Bible verse and rewrite practicing penmanship; discuss how language is unique to humans; read Genesis account of the confusion of languages; make map of the language groups in the world; discuss benefits of being multilingual; research how speech develops in babies; research speech therapy as a career.

Thursday: spell vocabulary words orally, take practice test; play the Stepping Hearts Game with new and old vocabulary; rewrite your sentences using different adjectives; continue research topic of interest and prepare short report; review week five and this week's study of senses/language.

Friday: play Jumping Bee Game to review spelling and definitions of words, take the spelling test; give reports/present experiments; have students give oral presentation on week's lesson content.

Lesson Plans Grades K-3 Week 8

Bible/ Religion Studies
Monday—Friday: teacher's selection of verses/lessons.

Teaching Outline
Monday: races; **Tuesday**: human history; **Wednesday**: human history, continued ;**Thursday**: review and preparation for presentations; **Friday**: reports and presentations

Language Arts/Math/Science/History/Music/Art

Monday: assign vocabulary words/write definitions on index cards; write words five times each; discuss races; make a family tree; look on map to locate where your family came from; interview family members and write the stories they tell.

Tuesday: use vocabulary words in sentence/write words five times each; begin making cards for the Stepping Hearts Game; discuss human history; take tour through history and view some of important inventions/buildings ancient man has accomplished.

Wednesday: write vocabulary words five times each/alphabetize the words; have older students include words from previous weeks; write or dictate your Bible verse and rewrite practicing penmanship; research an invention you are interested in learning about.

Thursday: spell vocabulary words orally/take practice test; play the Stepping Hearts Game with new and old vocabulary; work with picking out nouns and verbs and adjectives in your sentences; learn about adverbs; finish any projects/experiments/reports; continue recording heart rate/pulse rate.

Friday: play Jumping Bee Game to review spelling and definitions of words, take the spelling test.; present any reports/experiments for the week.

Reading List
K-3

*Books may be difficult to find in the library and some are no longer in print but you can find them on Amazon or eBay fairly easily and for great prices.

Oral or Silent Reading: (Depending on child's reading ability)

Drop of Blood by Paul Showers

     Publisher: Collins, 2004, 32pp. Discover the difference between red and white blood cells, circulation, and other fun facts about the blood presented on a third grade reading level.

Helen Keller by Lois Marken

     Publisher: Franklin Watts, 1993, 64pp. This book focuses on the high points of Helen's life. It is a good introduction and can be combined with a study of the senses and the problems associated with any handicap.

The Magic School Bus Inside the Human Body by Joanna Cole

     Publisher: Scholastic, 1990, 40pp. All of The Magic School Bus stories are unique! Take a fictional ride with the "teacher" inside of the human body. This book will help children understand the scientific vocabulary and a complicated subject in a fun way.

The Magic School Bus Inside Ralphie: A Book About Germs by John May & Jocelyn Stevenson

     Publisher: Scholastic, 1995, 30 pp. This book is adapted from the TV series. It leaves out a lot of the visual details (Mrs. Fizzle's dress! She wears the same one throughout the entire book!) along with some of the side bars (the "what is..." comments). It is obvious that this book was written by different authors. It does explain infection, white and red blood cells, antibiotics, and bacteria well.

Men of Science, Men of God by Henry M. Morris

Publisher: Master Books, 1988, 127 pp. Gives sixty-two biographical sketches of important scientists who believed in the Bible.

Why Does My Nose Run and Other Questions Kids Ask About Their Bodies by Joanne Settel and Nancy Baggett

Publisher: Ivy Books, 1989, 83 pp. A cute book featuring some "must know" answers such as the aforementioned title. This covers everything from why do I   sneeze, yawn, hiccup, to what are pimples, warts, skin color, headaches, to why does my stomach growl, etc. There are fifty-one questions listed in brief one-to-two page answers. Lots of interesting facts covered in an easy-to-understand way.

Activity and Experiment
Resource List
K-3

Here are resources that will be helpful in this study. These are my favorites; many more are listed in the Resource Section.

Biology for Every Kid by Janice VanCleave

Publisher: John Wiley & Sons, 1990, 240 pp. Has lots of great experiments dealing with the body that are easy to do. Best of all, the materials are easy to find.

Blood and Guts by Linda Allison

Publisher: Little, Brown and Company, 1976, 127 pp. A great book with lots of wonderful activities and experiments. This takes you through the whole body. The book details body functions in a clear and concise manner. It has wonderful ideas for many great experiments. Its best feature is details for dissection and observation of a bone, tooth, muscle, tendon and joint, heart (lamb's), kidney (lamb's), eye (sheep or beef), and brain (beef). If you want a basic book for younger grades dealing with dissections, I highly recommend it.

How the Body Works by Steve Parker

Publisher: Dorling Kindersley Publishers Ltd, 1999, 192 pp. If you must get only one book, this is the one to get. See if your library has it. It has beautiful pictures, explanations and lots of experiments and activities. Even if you don't do all the experiments, you can read about them. There are facts about scientists interspersed throughout. The only flaw is that it views life from an evolutionary perspective.

My Amazing Body: A First Book of Health and Fitness, by Pat   Thomas,
    Hauppauge, NY: Barron's, 2002

My Body by Patricia Carratello
    Publisher: Teacher Created Resources, 2004, 38 pp. It is charmingly hand printed and drawn. Make a "life size" outline of your child's body complete with body organs. Directions are included for copying, cutting, and coloring. Your child can then attach the organs to his "body." We did this when my children were little and kept it as room decoration for many years (I think we still have it somewhere!).

Your Insides, by Joanna Cole,
    New York, NY: Putnam and Grosset   Group, 1988, 1998, c 1992

Vocabulary/Spelling List
Grades K-3

These words may be used as a base for any vocabulary or spelling list. You may want to add more of your own once you begin studying this topic. Use the words as *vocabulary only* for the younger children.

artery	contract	large intestines	skin
backbone	diaphragm	liver	skull
bitter	digestion	lungs	small intestines
bladder	digestive system	nerve	sour
blood	energy	nose	spinal cord
blood cells	esophagus	mouth	spine
blood vessels	eyes	muscles	stomach
body	fat cells	plasma	sweet
bones	finger	red blood cells	taste buds
brain	gall bladder	respiratory	teeth
brain stem	germs	system	veins
breathing	heart	rib cage	vertebra
carbon dioxide	joints	ribs	voice box (larynx)
cells	kidneys	salt	waste
circulation	knee cap	senses	white blood cells
		skeleton	windpipe (trachea)

Vocabulary/Spelling
and Grammar Ideas
K-3

Use the vocabulary words as spelling words. Here are some activities to help you incorporate the vocabulary words into your unit study.

◊ Pick out some vocabulary words you would like your child to learn. Have him write them on index cards (or you write them) and have him put them in alphabetical order.

◊ Have children use the words in sentences to show the meaning. Younger children can use the words in sentences or stories. They can dictate the words to an adult or older child who can write the sentences for them. Then have them "read" their sentences.

◊ Have young children (K) pick out letters of the alphabet that they need to learn. Write the vocabulary words in large bold print on an erasable surface, or on paper. Have them circle the letter they are learning. (All the A's, B's, C's, etc.) Be sure to add your own **basic** words to the list! You can also use several lines from the Scripture (1 Corinthians 12:12-27) for this lesson.

◊ Choose one or two of the children's "best" sentences and have them recopy them using their neatest handwriting. (Give them a model to copy if they are just learning to print or write.)

◊ Use the sentences the child has written to label the parts of speech. Use colored pencils or markers for this activity. Color code each part of speech as follows:

   Underline the **nouns** once in red

Underline the **verbs** twice in blue

Draw a green squiggly line under the **adjectives**

Draw a purple box around the **prepositions**

(Continue this pattern with any other parts of speech you are studying.)

◊ Use the vocabulary words for younger children to make picture books. The children can cut pictures out of magazines or draw pictures to illustrate the words.

◊ Make up short rhymes. For example: "For my Jesus loved me so, he gave me a body that would _____ ." (grow)

◊ Have the child look in the grocery store for as many "body" words as possible, for example: "elbow" macaroni, "T-bone" steak, "life" savers, etc. Have the child keep an ongoing list of words, adding to them as each new item is found.

◊ Have spelling or vocabulary "jumping" bees. (If you have more than one child, give each one words from his own list.) Each child starts at one end of the room. If he defines the word correctly, or spells the word correctly, he can take one of the following: two baby jumps, a one-leg hop, three little steps, etc. (make up whatever you wish!). Children love this game. It's even a favorite with older kids. The child to reach the end first is the winner. (No-win version: the children compete against themselves, keeping track of words that are correct or incorrect.)

◊ Make "stepping hearts" using the vocabulary words. Take scrap paper, draw large "hearts," and write a vocabulary word on each sheet of paper. Spread the "hearts" out in a pattern on the floor. The child takes a pebble or other marker. Using dice, roll a number. The child takes the number of "steps" shown on the dice, then reads the word on the "heart" where he stops. If he defines the word correctly, he places his marker on the "heart". The first to finish wins. Game variations: winner is the one who answers the most words correctly.

◊ Fishing game: Cut out small fish in various shapes and label each with one of the vocabulary words. (Have the children help with this activity!) Clip a paper clip to each "fish". Tie a string to a magnet, and attach to a yardstick or dowel rod. Use the fishing rod to fish for words. The "fisherman" can keep the fish if he can give the correct definition, spell the word, or tell what part of speech it is. The one who has the most fish wins.

Language Arts Ideas
K-3

These suggestions may help you with incorporating language arts into your unit study. The more subjects you can naturally add to your study the easier you unit-study experience will be, and the flow will be cohesive. Children love learning when it makes sense and has purpose. Language Arts naturally works with learning new words, reading and using the Scriptures the child is learning to round out the study.

◊ Read The Magic School Bus Inside the Human Body. Have your child pretend he is a student in Miss Fizzle's class. What would he do or say on each page? Have him draw pictures of himself and write down his comments. Read the book again including his comments! (Do the same activity with any other book of interest.)

◊ Tape record the above activity with the additional dialogue and sound effects.

◊ Read 1 Corinthians 12:12-27. Write a portion of the Scripture on the board or a sheet of paper for him to copy in his best writing. Have him use this for a dramatic reading. He can memorize a line or two if he cannot read.

◊ Use different vocabulary words and their meanings. Inventing as many creative descriptions as possible, take turns describing a part of the body and have the others guess which part it is.

◊ Have each child write a paper telling about his life as a doctor. Have him tell why he chose this profession and what his greatest "experience" has been.

◊ Begin an open-ended story, and take turns adding to the story orally (this is especially fun with a group of different-aged children). For example: "It was a beautiful spring day and my family was taking a walk in _____ Park. I was leading the way with my (brother, sister, friend) and was pretty far ahead when I noticed drops of blood on the path. I called back for my parents, but they were nowhere in sight. I looked at my (brother's, sister's, friend's) leg and noticed the blood was coming from a cut on ___'s knee. Since I always carried my first aid kit with me, I opened up my backpack and... "

◊ Use the above story with different variations. The places can be any of the geographical places you are studying. For example: While in the Rocky Mountains, Florida, California, etc.

◊ Write a paper naming all of the major parts of the body: heart, brain, lungs, stomach, intestines, liver, kidneys, etc. and a brief description of each one.

◊ Go on a field trip to a hospital. Observe the sights and sounds going on around you. Try to answer these questions after your trip. How many patients can stay at the hospital at one time? How many doctors and nurses are on staff? What are the different types of doctors? Is the hospital arranged in a special way? Where is the emergency room? What is the difference in people who are admitted to the hospital through the emergency room or through the admitting room? What is the fancy word used instead of "admitting room"? What are some of the reasons people need a hospital? Write a paper detailing what you saw. (Some of these suggestions were taken from *Indoor Trips That Teach.*)

◊ Have your child keep a diary of any illness. Record things he had to do to get well. Did he have to eat special foods, rest, or take medicine? Write the names of medicine taken and observe the ingredients. What are these ingredients? Can these words be found in a dictionary? If not, where? (Medical dictionary, doctor's office, college library.) Parents or older siblings can write for the younger child, or give him a tape recorder to record his findings.

◊ Write a poem or rhyme about the body. Write a variation of an original poem or song, substituting vocabulary from this study. Example: "Mouth, mouth, teeth and gums are only what we see, but when the food goes down your tum it makes you strong you see..." (To the tune of *Row, Row, Row Your Boat.*)

◊ Write about taking a trip into inner space. How did you get there? What did you take? Where did you go? What did you see? How fast did you travel? How did you get out?

◊ Make your own crossword puzzle. Write definitions for the vocabulary words. Give to an older sibling or parent to figure out.

◊ Choose a paragraph from one of the books you are reading on anatomy. Write this paragraph neatly and have the children copy it. Dictate the paragraph to older children once they have learned to spell the words. Have them check their own papers. (This may need to be practiced more than once.)

◊ Find some places in Scripture that deal with the body. What could you look under to find these places? Write several passages and choose one to copy neatly. Frame it and hang it up! Don't forget to write chapter and verse.

◊ The word "hair" is used in many different ways. Can you think up words or phrases that use "hair" in them? For example: hairdresser, hairline, to split hairs etc. (*Look at Hair*)

Math Reinforcement
Ideas

◊ Have the children organize the parts of the body (heart, brain, hand, lungs, foot, legs, teeth, mouth, fingers, eyes, ears, etc.) from smallest to largest.

◊ Have your child add some equations using his fingers. For example, four plus two. Have him do several different problems. Then give him a sheet of five problems. Have him time how long it takes him to add these problems, again using his fingers. Now have him memorize the answers and re-take the test, timing himself. Which is quicker?

◊ Estimate the number of miles of veins we have. How many zeros are in the number? Can anyone walk that far? Why not? Walk one mile. How long did it take? How long does it take by car? Compare the various times.

◊ How many miles of blood vessels do we have? Write down this number. How many zeros are there? What is the place value of each of the various digits?

◊ Have your child carefully measure his height when he first wakes up. Measure it again later in the day. Are there any changes? Why? (Blood and Guts)

◊ Show the concept of multiplication (or sets) by grouping. Fold one sheet of paper in quarters, draw large red "platelets" and cut out. Group them in sets of 2, 3, 4, etc. Is it easier to multiply or add?

◊ Show the concept of division by breaking up groups of "platelets" (or use *heart* shaped candies or candy kisses) by dividing the numbers evenly among several people. (Character trait of generosity!)

◊ Make a body to scale. Use a ruler with precise measurements and have your child draw an outline of his body on a large sheet of paper. Convert the inches to centimeters.

◊ During a trip to the doctor's (dentist, etc.) office count the number of chairs, people, books, magazines, etc. in the waiting room. Make a chart of each when you get home. Draw a graph showing each amount. Which items were the most abundant? Which was the least?

◊ How many times does a heart beat per minute? To find out, have your child check his pulse (the carotid artery on your neck is a good place). Have him place his fingertips on his neck just below his jawbone. Count the number of pulses for thirty seconds and multiply this number by two. Record this number.

◊ Have your child do the above activity after exercising, running, jumping rope, or skipping. Record his pulse for one minute. How does it compare to his resting pulse rate? Chart the results. Do this with other family members and chart all the results. Who has the lowest or highest reading? Do kids or adults have faster pulses? Why?

◊ Count calories and fat grams of your favorite foods. Look at the label and chart which foods are highest in the following: fat, sugar, carbohydrates, calories, cholesterol, sodium, protein, and minerals. Do any of these foods (try cereals) contain vitamins, such as; Vitamin A, Vitamin C, Thiamine, Riboflavin, Niacin, Calcium, or Iron?

◊ What are your measurements? Draw an outline of your body on a sheet of paper and using a measuring tape (have someone help you) measure the different parts. Some suggestions are: feet, waist, legs, arms, wrist, head, neck, torso (trunk), and whatever else you wish to measure. Use inches or meters. Make a chart of your findings.

◊ Take your temperature at different times during the day. Make a chart of the results. Write down the time of day and the temperature that was measured. How does your body temperature change? Why?

◊ What is your child's reaction time? (The time it takes for his brain to process instructions relating to an action his body must perform.) Do this activity with two people. How quickly can your child catch a ruler (or any object) another person drops in front of him? The faster he react the less time the ruler has to fall. Estimate where his hand will be on the ruler. At the top, in the middle, or at the lower end? Can this reaction time improve with practice? Have him do this ten times. Chart and graph his results.

◊ Does your chest expand when you breathe? Have your child breathe in deeply and measure his chest. Now, have him exhale and measure his chest. What is the difference?

◊ Time how long your child can hold his breath. (There is a limit because of a built in automatic response that will cause him to breathe.)

Science Activities and Experiments
K-3

Doing science activities and experiments is lots of fun! Using the scientific method makes it easier to understand. The *scientific method* is a procedure used to do an experiment in an organized fashion. The point of the scientific method is to solve a problem or further investigate an observation. Once you ask the question make sure the children give you their *hypothesis* (or "guess" for the younger children). This is what they think will happen. If they have no idea, read or observe to further research the question. The children can write (or draw) their experiment using the scientific method sheets found in this book. *Parental supervision necessary! Always use caution when doing any science projects or experiments. After using raw meats always wash your hands and surrounding areas with anti-bacterial soap!*

◊ Squeeze a tennis ball. The force needed to squeeze a tennis ball is like the force needed to squeeze blood out of the heart. Measure your child's pulse rate (for example, sixty-six times per minute). Squeeze the tennis ball that amount of times. Can you imagine how hard your heart works in one hour? One day?

◊ Have your child make a stethoscope (many science books have directions—see *Blood and Guts* or *How the Body Works*). Have him listen to the sounds of his heart. Why does your heart make different sounds? Where does the blood go? Have him draw a picture of his body and the heart with arrows showing the direction of the blood flow.

◊ Do a dissection (web addresses are given in the resource section). If you don't want to dissect an object, (you are my kind of person) you can view different organs on a interactive websites online. Please use your discretion when viewing online sites with keywords of the "body" and make sure you have your safe search settings set.

◊ How strong are bones? Save chicken bones (thigh or leg bones are needed) after a meal (you can also use the wishbone and reduce the time by seven to ten days). Have your children put the bone in a large glass container that can be sealed with a lid. Pour white wine vinegar (a weak acid) into the jar covering the bone. Allow to sit for two to three weeks undisturbed. Pour out the vinegar and rinse the bone in water. What happened to the bone? (By removing the mineral salts and reducing the bone to its underlying cartilage material, you should be able to bend the bone as if it is rubber!) This experiment can be done overnight by using a stronger 6% hydrochloric or muriatic acid (used in pools). This must be done by adults only; that's why I prefer the other experiment for children. Rinse the bones in a solution of one cup of water and three to four teaspoons of baking soda before allowing the children to handle the bone.) Encourage your children to consume lots of calcium!

◊ Obtain soup bones and look at the marrow and other parts of the bone. Meats such as pork chops have bone marrow in them. Save teeth that have fallen out. Have your child use one for the following experiment. Take your child's favorite type of soft drink and place it into a glass container with a lid. Drop the tooth into the soft drink and check it twice a week. What happens to the tooth? Keep a diary of this. Have younger children draw what they see. (Scientific Method sheet)

◊ Cut a sliver from a piece of raw steak (or chicken). Place it on a clean surface and use a sharp instrument (a dissecting tool or pointed ice pick) to slowly pull apart the muscle fibers. Place them on a microscope slide, or thin glass surface. (Improvise with the materials you have on hand.) Use a microscope or a hand magnifying lens (won't work as well) to view the muscle fibers . Record what you find. You can put a few drops of a homemade stain that will help you see the fibers better. (See page 150) *Note: Always wash hands and surfaces thoroughly with soap and water after handling raw meat.

◊ Make a pulse meter. Take a small ball of clay (the size of a large marble) and a match stick (or toothpick, taking off the tip to make a dull edge). Place the clay on your wrist, trying to find your pulse. Put the match stick in the clay. Observe the match stick. What happens?

◊ Has your child (or you!) had a cut or scraped knee lately? The next time you do, observe the injury. What happens to the wound once the bleeding is stopped? How long does it take to clot or for a scab to form? Why does this happen?

◊ Have your child do tests for starch or fat. To test for starch use iodine and different types of food (such as bread or a slice of raw potato). Place a drop of iodine on each item. If it turns blue-black it has starch in it. Test for fat by cutting up squares from a brown paper bag. Rub different foods (French fries or mayonnaise) on the squares of paper and let it dry. Hold it up to the light, and if there is fat on it, the light will shine through. Make a chart of the different foods and two columns with starch and fat at the top of each. Mark which foods fall into these categories.

◊ Have your child chew a salty cracker well without swallowing it for several minutes. How does it taste? Did the taste change from salty to sweet? Why? (Because the enzymes in his mouth break down the starch into a sugar.) When he swallows, have him feel his neck. Can he feel his "Adam's apple"?

◊ Take a piece of raw chicken, a thigh with the leg attached. Examine it to see how joints work and observe the muscles that are attached.

◊ Have your child stand in front of a mirror with his shirt off (girls can do this privately!), have him raise his arms above his head and breathe in deeply. Have him watch the outline of his rib cage.

◊ Experiment with different tastes. Blindfold the child and have him hold his nose. Rub bits of different types of foods on his tongue for several seconds. Can he identify the food? Write down his answers. Now repeat the experiment without holding his nose. Is it easier to identify the food? How important is the sense of smell? How does this relate to the taste food has when you have a cold?

◊ Use a shoe box with a lid and cut a hole in one end large enough to slip a hand in. Have one person place an object inside and place the lid on. Have another person to feel the object without looking. How many objects can he identify? Do this same activity again, only this time have the child wear gloves. Can he still identify the items easily?

◊ Place a hand mirror into the refrigerator for one hour. Wipe the surface and have your child hold it up to his face and breathe on it. What happens?

(The vapor in his breath condenses as a fog of droplets on the mirror surface). (*How the Body Works*)

◊ Observe how uniquely God made us by fingerprinting each child. Make a pencil smudge by shading a two-inch square until there is a layer of graphite. Have your child rub his index finger into the graphite and place a piece of clear tape over the darkened finger. Remove the tape and stick it on a sheet of typing paper. Repeat this process until all of the fingers are done. Observe the patterns with a magnifying glass. Have several children do this activity. Are any of the prints the same?

◊ Make a map of your tongue. Take different foods: orange juice, banana, salt, crackers, etc. Using a Q-tip, dab one end into the food and onto your tongue. Try the same food in different places on the tongue. Try the front tip, left side, left side back, back, right side front and right side back. The different parts of the tongue taste sweet, salty, sour and bitter.

◊ Make a chart of the senses. Label the top with pictures of a hand, nose, ear, eye, and mouth. On one side cut out (or draw) pictures of everyday objects, such as, books, food items, animals, vehicles, etc. Place a check under the senses used to "experience" the item. For example, you would use your eyes and hands to look at a book. If the book was read aloud, you would use your ears.

◊ Make your muscles work. Do some exercises (sit-ups, etc.). How long can you do exercises until you become tired? Why do you get tired? Make a chart (ideally over a several week period) and chart how many of each chosen exercise you can do before you get tired. What happens over a period of several weeks? Why does this happen?

Geography/History
Ideas
K-3

◊ Make a world map using large sheets of paper (computer paper taped together works well). Many newspaper companies sell newspaper remnant rolls for a minimal charge ($1.00). Use pieces of yarn to outline the continents. Place a star on countries where your ancestors lived. How many generations removed are you from those ancestors? Make a family tree.

◊ Using the above map, locate and mark places where early scientists such as Andreas Vesalius (born in Belgium, worked in Italy), Robert Hooke (England), Marcello Malpighi and Camillo Golgi (Italy) Wilhelm Röntgen (Germany), René Descartes (France), William Beaumount and Ernest Starling (United States), Karl Landsteirner (Australia) , Herman von Helmholtz (Germany), and Antony van Leeuwenhoek (Netherlands) lived. (Scientists found in *How the Body Works)*

◊ Study and read about the different scientists and doctors that made major discoveries. Talk about their contributions. You can do a mini-play; pretend you are the scientist telling another person about a great discovery. Perhaps you are the first person the scientist told about his discovery. Tell how he acted, and whether he was excited. Do this with several people.

◊ How did early discoveries and books, such as *The Fabric of the Human Body* by Andreas Vealius in 1543, affect the thoughts of the day? Why were people affected? (Until that time no one had done extensive research or documented the inside of the body.)

◊ How was the microscope discovered? Who made this discovery? Did other scientists contribute to this discovery?

◊ Who were the first people mentioned in the *Bible*? Can you draw a chart of the people that were mentioned after the first two? How far can you go?

◊ Who's "family" was Jesus descended from? Why was this so important in the time of Jesus? Why is this important today?

◊ What were different unsuccessful techniques used to try to cure people? For example, for high fever they often would "bleed" the sick person to let the "bad" blood flow out. When did this practice begin? When did it stop?

◊ Who discovered the fact that germs spread? How did this discovery help? What were early illnesses that spread called? (Epidemics) What was the effect on the people of the day when an epidemic spread? Who took care of the sick people? Why?

◊ What is an "Achilles' heel"? What country did the saying originate from? Who was Achilles?

◊ How did food and living conditions historically affect the body in relation to height? In relation to life span?

◊ What effect did the discovery of penicillin have on people? How was it discovered?

Art/Music
K-3

Art

◊ Draw a life-size picture of yourself. Put in all of your facial features, hair and skin coloring and favorite outfit. Don't forget your ears or eyebrows! (You may also want to draw another outline with your inside parts labeled.)

◊ Make different molds of your hands, fingers, feet, (or anything else you wish!). **Recipe for clay dough:** four cups of flour, one cup of salt, one and one half cups of water. Add more flour if it's too sticky. Knead six minutes. Shape, then bake at 325°-350° until slightly brown.

◊ Make a 3-D model of your teeth. Dry your teeth with a paper towel. Use plasticine clay. Shape a thick piece of clay to fit your mouth. Bite into the clay and press it up against your teeth to make a good impression. Carefully pull it away. (If the clay breaks apart, do it again with another piece that is thicker.) Do both the upper and lower jaws. Tape a strip of paper (poster) around the edge of the mold. Now mix 3/4 of a cup of Plaster of Paris and enough water to make a creamy liquid. Pour into the mold and tap it lightly to make sure the plaster went down into the grooves. When the plaster is dry, (at least two to three hours more time if it is a humid day in Florida!) carefully remove the clay. Write your name and date on this.

◊ Make a model of history from the beginning of time (use the *Bible* to help you with a time line). Use pieces of poster board and draw out the days of Creation. Pay special attention to when the people were created! Use yarn or string to hang your pictures up.

◊ Draw pictures (or cut out pictures from a magazine) of the different stages of life: infancy, one year, five, ten, fifteen, twenty, and sixty. (Or any combination of years you wish). If you can find pictures of yourself, use one from each year and make a poster.

◊ Make thumb print art. Use a waterproof ink pad and carefully ink your thumb. Place your finger on a sheet of paper and make a print. When it dries, use this as the basis of a "body," and draw a head, arms, legs and feet. Use your other fingers and make a family of fingerprints.

◊ Make a body apron. Use a chef's apron (one that ties on the neck and waist) or sew one. Make body organs out of construction paper or pieces of felt. Attach with Velcro where they belong on your body.

Music

◊ Sing along with *Wee Sing Bible Songs*. Note how many songs deal with Creation and the body. How many songs can be done with hand and body movements? (Variation: *Wee Sing Children's Songs)*

◊ Record the sounds of various body functions, such as your heart beat, the hiccups, a sneeze or cough, or a stomach when it is growling. Use a microphone and tape recorder. Which sounds are the loudest? Why?

◊ Do "finger plays". Devise your own to go with different songs. Try to use different parts of the body.

◊ Make a water scale. Take the same size glasses and place different amounts of water in each one. Place them in order from the glass with the least amount of water first, to the glass with the most water last. Try to use eight glasses, one for each note of the scale. Lightly tap on the side of the glass with a spoon. Play a song!

◊ Can you make a musical instrument with your hands? Clasp your hands together placing your thumbs side-by-side. Try to blow through the space between your thumbs. Experiment with different ways to hold your thumbs and purse your lips.

◊ Use a rubber band and place it around your index finger and thumb. Gently pull on the band and watch it vibrate. Try different thicknesses of rubber bands. What sounds do they make? (Variation: try this with a shoe box and string rubber bands to make your own instrument.)

◊ Sing. Press your finger gently on the front of your throat; feel the vibrations of your vocal cords.

◊ Can you whistle? Practice whistling or watch someone who can and ask him to teach you. Watch the way to hold your lips. What do you do with your tongue? How do you blow? Try to whistle a tune.

◊ Sing or play *Onward Christian Soldiers* and march to the music.

◊ Sing or play songs relating to the body using hand and leg motions. Some suggested songs are *He's Got the Whole World in His Hands, Head and*

Shoulders, Just as I Am. Add any others you can think of that include the body.

◊ Sing or play *There is Victory in Jesus, There is Power in the Blood,* and an all-time favorite, *Jesus Loves Me, This I Know.*

Creation Anatomy Outline
Grades 4-8

I. Body Analogy

A. Scripture: 1 Corinthians 12:12-27

B. Value of Materials

C. Price paid

II. Circulatory System

A. Scriptures

B. Definitions

C. Heart

D. Blood Parts

F. Lungs and Breathing

III. Injuries and Healing

A. Blood Cells

    1. Red Blood Cells

    2. White Blood Cells

    3. Platelets

B. Immunity

    1. Lymph system

    2. Bacteria and Viruses

    3. How Science catches up with the Bible

IV. Skeletal System and Muscles

A. Framework

    1. Construction

    2. Function

B. Muscles

    1. How they work

    2. Type

C. Joints

D. Hands

V. Digestive System

A. Mouth

B. Teeth

C. Salvia

D. Esophagus

F. Liver

B. Small Intestines

C. Large Intestines

D. Kidneys

VI. Nervous System and the Brain

VII. Reproductive System

VIII. DNA

IX. Senses
A. Eye
B. Ear
C. Taste
Language

XI. Races

XII. Human History

Lesson Plans

Subject Date:	Monday	Tuesday	Wednesday	Thursday	Friday
Bible/Religion Studies					
Teaching Outline					
Reading Section					
Language Arts/Spelling/ Vocabulary					
Math Reinforcement					
Science Activities and Experiments					
Geography/History					
Art/Music					

CR= Creation Resource   TS= Teacher Selection

Lesson Plans Grades 4-8 Week 1

Bible/ Religion Studies

Monday –Wednesday Cor. 12:12-27 (dictation / memory work)**Thursday-Friday** Lev 17:4 Gen 2:7 and verses of your choice dealing with blood/heart / breathe. Show how to use a Bible Concordance to find other related verses.

Morning warm up: 5 minute write up. Do this everyday and you will be surprise how quickly you kids will love it! This is a great way to get past writer's block. Anything they write in 5 minutes is shared at the end. Here's how it works: Give your student 5 minutes to write something about a topics that you choose—what ever comes into your head. Here's what is popping into my head right now, for example: how or if a foot can get along without the rest of the body or how is your body unique, or what is your favorite body part and why or what do you want to learn about the body, or how do you think food effects the body, or how can you make a body stronger or grow taller or faster or can you? This is just a quick exercise and the children will get better and better at it every day. They don't ponder the topic they just pick up their pen/pencil and write. My kids balked at first, but by the end of the first week, they were begging for more time to finish! They wrote short stories, poems, songs and many silly sentences! It doesn't matter the point is to get the creative juices flowing and to get it on paper! (Additional 5 minute write-up ideas: heart, love, sacrifice, obedience, medicine, feet, exercise, doctor, emergency, experiment, determination, breathe)

Teaching Outline– Monday: I- a, b,c, II-a,b,c **Tuesday** –Review II-d **Wednesday**- II d,e **Thursday**-II-Review **Friday** –Review knowledge II a,b,c,d,e

Reading/Research—Everyday. Reading 30 minutes –1 hour (perhaps even longer depending on the research you are asking them to do) everyday both silently and aloud. Choose books with your children that will explore Circulation and Respiration Systems. See reading list. Consider looking for biographies of men and women who contributed to the science/medical fields like: Christian Barnard, William Harvey, Carlos Finlay, Walter Reed, Hippocrates so you can include some historical/ geographical perspectives and subject integration into this unit study.

Language Arts/Vocabulary:

Monday: assign vocabulary using list (look for words dealing with this section of the Teaching Outline) adding words from your own resources as needed for spelling and definition work. Have students keep a vocabulary words and definitions on index in a card file. It makes daily quick reviews easy; Re-write the

Scripture verses using their own words. Do some sentence diagraming of these sentences. Do this activity throughout unit– Make Trivia Cards

Tuesday: Review vocabulary words learning the spelling and reviewing the definitions; Find sentences in your books using 5 words and do some sentence diagraming. Dictate 2-3 sentences from one of your books using your vocabulary.

Wednesday: Practice spelling words by writing lists with some words misspelled; Make a hopscotch and learn vocabulary definitions (Spelling, Vocabulary and Grammar Ideas 4-8).

Thursday: Write an open ended story using your vocabulary words—did you spell them correctly and use them correctly in context?

Friday: Take a spelling test; orally ask the definitions; Ask comprehension questions about the books the student is reading and have the student read several pages aloud.

Math Reinforcement/Science Activities and Experiments/Geography/History/ Art/Music/Drama– Using your resources both in this guide and those you have found in the library, bookstores, and internet put together your students integrated curriculum plan of attack! Remember: Read it; watch it (or follow the processes by a diagram); review it; have the student tell it back to you orally and in writing, drawing or modeling projects. Ask yourself and your student what they want to learn and what interests them most. If you are writing papers of any length assign them early in the week to allow time to read, take notes and put the paper together. Choose different types of writing too- poetry, reviews, consider more dramatic options like a informational advertisements about heart disease, or asthma using sound effects like heart beat and breathing.

Monday: Using the Teaching Outline Read/Teach from the outline about the value both spiritually and materially of the Human Body. Watch the Red River of Life DVD as an introduction. Discuss the movie and write a review; Make word problems from the mathematical data given about the material worth of the body provided in the Teaching Outline (Math Reinforcements 4-8). Spend extra time beginning to read your resource books and the books chosen to be read individually. Take pulse after different exercises (PE/ Math) Use the chart and redo the exercises daily to monitor changes in pulse rate during the unit.

Tuesday: Read/Teach from the outline about the blood and heart. If you want, watch the Red River of Life DVD again. What did you see/learn this time that you missed yesterday? Make and label drawings of the heart and have the student explain how the blood passes through the heart (Science/Art) Have your students explain the path blood takes through the heart, lung, heart. Take pulse after different exercises (PE/ Math). Using the Scientific Method sheet, do the osmosis experiment. (Janice VanCleave's Biology for Every Kid also has some experiments dealing with osmosis and diffusion) Use the Teaching Outline to make Trivia Cards. Make up a game using the cards.

Wednesday: Check and complete your observations on the osmosis experiment and record the information on your Scientific Method sheet. What process does oxygen go through after it is inhaled? Explain the process. Play your Trivia Card Game to review. Learn about blood pressure and have your blood pressure taken. Have your teacher donate blood and go watch the process and interview the phlebotomist. Write a news article about the importance of blood donation. (Language Arts) How many times do you breathe in and out? Record sound effect of heart and breathing using them in an informational advertisement about heart and lung diseases. Try to get different animal hearts from the Butcher to compare, cut in half and identify the chambers.

Thursday: Teaching Outline -Respiration process. Check your resources for building model lungs and demonstrating respiration. How many breathes do you take in one day? (Math), Graph the proportion of gases in the Air. If your student is reading a biography of a scientist/doctor create a timeline of what is happening during that time history. How does history impact his research, thoughts. (History) Find his country, where he traveled on a globe. (Geography). Add cards to the Trivia Game.

Friday: Play the Trivia Game to review what you have learned. Consider watching the Red River of Life once again to reinforce the information and learning that has taken place. Did you learn anything new? How is hearing and seeing this information different than the first time you watched it? Give oral presentations using the charts, graph, diagrams and drawing to explain the circulation and respiration system. Find poems about the body. Act out the advertisement. How best can your student recap what learning has taken place?

Lesson Plans Grades 4-8 Week 2

Bible/ Religion Studies—Teacher's choice of verses and lessons

Morning warm up: 5 minute write up! A few quick ideas— but let YOUR imagination go and think of some of your own starters: scar, sneeze, skinned knees, red, stitches, germs, shots

Teaching Outline-Monday-Review, III-a1-3 **Tuesday-**III-b1 **Wednesday-**III-b2,3 **Thursday**– Review, **Friday**– reports and presentations

Reading/Research—Every day: Reading 30 minutes to one hour everyday both silently and aloud. Check comprehension/ review note cards

Language Arts, Spelling, Vocabulary:

Monday: Assign words and writing definitions on index cards, write each word 5 times;

Tuesday: Use the words in a sentence, write words 5 times each.

Wednesday: write words 5 times each alphabetize the words; write the harder words several in row with only one spelled correctly and see if student can pick out the correct spelling (Spelling, Vocabulary and Grammar Ideas 4-8). Select a paragraph for dictation and sentence diagraming (Spelling and Grammar Ideas 4-8).

Thursday: spell words orally, take practice test; Begin an open-ended story (Language Arts Ideas 9-12) or write a short story entitled " A day in the Life of a Blood Cell" (Language Arts Ideas 4-8)

Friday: Review, check spelling and grammar, practice reading aloud for flow of chapter; read it to your younger siblings; take the spelling test.

Math Reinforcement/Science Activities and Experiments/Geography/History/ Art/Music/Drama:

Monday: Review material from last week especially pertaining to blood cells; add more Trivia Cards; Continue with the exercise program started last week: keep record of your heart rate; Continue to read books on our unit and assign appropriate ways to report what they are learning. If it is a biography, for history/ geography integration check a map or globe for where the scientist lived and what was happening in history at the time of his work. Make a life size drawing of your body and put in the organs studied (Art/Music K-3). Study a cut or scrape of someone in your home and monitor of the healing process. (Science Activities and Experiments K-3)Where are the blood cells made? What are the functions of each type of blood cell. Draw these cells and tell how they differ? How are the platelets different? How and why are platelets used in cancer treatment? Begin deeper research on a topic of interest concerning blood: hemophilia, leukemia, etc.

Tuesday: Add the lymph system to your body drawing; What immunizations have you had? Look at your immunization card can you explain the entries? What does Bible say about diseases and cleanliness. Prepare cleanliness survey (Math Reinforcement Ideas 4-8). Write copy for a commercial or public service announcement about the importance of getting a flu shot, or about some other health issue. Think of sound effects to put with the copy. What are some diseases of the lymph system? A growing number of people have stopped getting immunizations for their children. What are the repercussions of this? Choose a side of this controversial issue and research it. Determine how you want to present the information: speech, commercial, or written paper.

Wednesday: What is the difference between bacteria and virus. Grow bacteria. Who discovered penicillin? What can you discover about him and how he made this discovery. Research Louis Pasteur and his "germ theory." Where did he come from? What is spontaneous generation? (Science Activities and Experiments 9-12) Who are the other scientists who contributed to the creation of antibiotics and vaccines. Research Borelli burgdorferi (lymes disease); continue to work on your PSA. Can you film it?

Thursday: Continue to research your topics and decide how to present them tomorrow. Make Trivia Cards.

Friday: Play the Trivia Game for a review; make a presentation of your PSA, your speech, or paper and /or watch the video you made. Present results of any experiment done. Present orally or in writing any private readings that pertain to this part of the study.

Lesson Plans Grades 4-8 Week 3

Bible/ Religion Studies— Job 10: 8-11; Teacher's choice of verses and lessons

Morning warm up: 5 minute write up! A few quick ideas— but let YOUR imagination go and think of some of your own starters: bones, movement, muscles, joints, run, stretch, play;

Teaching Outline-Monday-IV-a, b **Tuesday-**IV-b1, b2 **Wednesday-**IV-c, d **Thursday–** IV d, review **Friday–** reports and presentations

Reading—Every day: Reading 30 minutes to one hour everyday both silently and aloud. Check comprehension/ review note cards.

Language Arts, Spelling, Vocabulary:

Monday: assign words and writing definitions on index cards, write each word 5 times.

Tuesday: use the words in a sentence, write words 5 times each; Play vocabulary Hopscotch (Spelling Vocabulary and Grammar Ideas 4-8).

Wednesday: write words 5 times each alphabetize the words; write the harder words several in row with only one spelled correctly and see if student can pick out the correct spelling. Select a paragraph for dictation and sentence diagraming.

Thursday: spell words orally, take practice test; Write basic sentences using the vocabulary word and let student add descriptive words. Research how electrical pulses are used in aiding people who have lost limbs.

Friday: Review, take the spelling test. Prepare a speech based on the research you did Thursday.

Math Reinforcement/Science Activities and Experiments/Geography/History/ Art/Music/Drama.

Monday: Are you still exercising and monitoring your heart rates, logging them in to your charts? Go over the information you have read in the books you have selected about the skeletal system and muscular system. Pull out the experiments you want to include and possibly already have started. (See Science Activities and Experiments for K– 3 with the chicken bones) Check out Blood and Guts by Linda Allison for several experiments. Check your other resources. Add some of the larger bones to your body drawing. Bones get some strength from their cylindrical shape. Demonstrate this (Science Activities and Experiments for grades 9-12). Why are the bones like this? How do you keep your bones strong? What happens when minerals are removed from bone (Science Activities and Experiments K-3).

Tuesday: Review what was learned about bones, How many? What are some of the major bones names? What are the bones function? Name the parts of the bone and what is marrow? Take a look at some soup bones to see the marrow. Ask what happens in the marrow of our bones. Research the number of bones in the bodies of different aged people. What does the word mouse have to do with muscle? Make a drawing or find a picture of the different types of muscles. How do the muscles differ from each other. Build a model of the arm (Science Activities and Experiments 4-8) or in Linda Allison's Blood and Guts are other suggestion on building the model arm. Explain how the muscles make the arm move (extend and contract). How long does it take for your muscles to tire? (Science Activities and Experiments 4-8)

Wednesday: How strong are you? Use the bathroom scale and record which part of your body is most powerful. (Math Reinforcement Ideas 4-8) Check out Easy Hands-on Models that Teach, by Donald M. Silver –the joints. What is a tendon and ligament? How long does it take for your muscles to tire (Science Activities for grades 4-8) Look up scientist Luigi Galvani, Alessandro Volta, and Sir Humphrey Davy and find out what they discovered about the human body, muscles and how they work. Where was each scientist from and find it on a map/globe. Who invented the first prosthetic device? Where were they from? Look up and report on the advances in technology in this area.

Thursday: Finish up models and experiments. Do a dissection of muscle tissue and examine the joints of a raw piece of chicken. Feel the tendons and muscles in your arm while holding a large can of vegetables (Science Activities and Experiments 4-8). Prepare presentations for Friday.

Friday: Update Trivia Game with new vocabulary, and play the Trivia Game for a review; make a presentation orally of private readings that pertain to this part of the study. Present data and results of any experiment done, explaining the scientific method. Demonstrate the model arm.

Lesson Plans Grades 4-8 Week 4

Bible/ Religion Studies— Genesis 1:29-30 Teacher's choice of verses and lessons

Morning warm up: 5 minute write up! A few quick ideas— but let YOUR imagination go and think of some of your own starters: stomach, enzymes, swallow, chew, favorite food, choke, fasting

Teaching Outline-Monday: V-a, b, c **Tuesday**-V-d, e, f **Wednesday**-V-g. h, i **Thursday**: Review **Friday**: reports and presentations

Reading: Every day: Reading 30 minutes to one hour everyday both silently and aloud. Check comprehension/ review note cards of research for book reports or oral reports

Language Arts, Spelling, Vocabulary:

Monday: assign words and writing definitions on index cards, write each word 5 times.

Tuesday: use the words in a sentence, write words 5 times each.

Wednesday: write words 5 times each alphabetize the words; write the harder words several in row with only one spelled correctly and see if student can pick out the correct spelling. Select a paragraph for dictation and sentence diagraming.

Thursday: spell words orally, take practice test; Write basic sentences using the vocabulary words and let student add descriptive words. (See Spelling, Vocabulary, and Grammar Ideas: 4-8)

Friday: Review, take the spelling test. Take five or six sentences from a book you are reading and answer the five "W's." (See Language Arts Ideas 4-8)

Math Reinforcement/Science Activities and Experiments/Geography/History/Art/Music/Drama-

Monday: Read through the section on Digestive System and make your plan of study and what area students want to dig deeper so that research starts today! For example the liver is a most amazing organ because it can repair itself if damaged! From your books read about the mouth, tongue, saliva, teeth and what happens when you bite into an apple or bagel. Discuss the concept of food as fuel and why eating good food is important, especially fruits and vegetables. (Gen. 1:29-30)

Go through the process of chewing food well and how food is broken down in our mouths with the help of saliva. Using a tooth, place it in a cup of soft drink and observe (Science Activities and Experiments K-4). Use your Scientific Method sheet to record out come of experiment over the week. If you have a dentist's appointment, have the student compile some interviewing questions to ask either the doctor or hygienist and then write a report about the visit. Diagram the inside of the mouth. Note where the saliva glands are. Add teeth to your body drawing. Make a 3-D model of your teeth. (See Art/Music K-3)

Tuesday: Add the Esophagus, stomach and liver to your body drawing. Check your resource books for experiments, like Janice Van Cleave's The Human Body for Everykid, for ideas and experiments or Easy Models that Teach. Measure the amount of food your eat in a day. (See Math Reinforcement Ideas 4-8) What foods give you the most energy? (See Science Activities and Experiments: 4 -8) Research the uniqueness of the liver or the way the ideas of healthy eating has changed since the Middle Ages and prepare a presentation for Friday (Geography/History Ideas 9-12).

Wednesday: Add the Small Intestine, Large Intestine, and Kidneys to your life-size body drawing. If you lay out the intestines how long are they? Continue to work on the experiments and models you have selected and be sure to prepare in writing or for oral presentation of the learning that has taken place. Research how food and living conditions affect the body in relation to height? (See Geography and History Ideas 4-8) Be prepared to share the information in some way on Friday.

Thursday: Add cards to your Trivia Game. Finish working on projects and reports for presentations on Friday.

Friday: Make presentations and reports, show models and experiments data and result as per the Scientific Method Sheets.

Lesson Plans Grades 4-8 Week 5

Bible/ Religion Studies— Phil. 4: 8 Teacher's choice of verses and lessons

Morning warm up: 5 minute write up! A few quick ideas— but let YOUR imagination go and think of some of your own starters: brain, smart, intelligence, imagine, dream, understanding, balance.

Teaching Outline: Monday: Parts of the Brain, Cerebrum (largest part), cerebellum (balance) **Tuesday**– Pituitary gland, Brainstem (involuntary activities), hypothalamus, thalamus **Wednesday**-Nerves **Thursday**– Review **Friday**– reports and presentations.

Reading—Every day: Read 30 minutes to one hour everyday both silently and aloud. Check comprehension/ review note cards of research for book reports or oral reports

Language Arts, Spelling, Vocabulary:

Monday: assign words and writing definitions on index cards, write each word 5 times.

Tuesday: use the words in a sentence, write words 5 times each.

Wednesday: write words 5 times each alphabetize the words; write the harder words several in row with only one spelled correctly and see if student can pick out the correct spelling. Select a paragraph for dictation and sentence diagraming.

Thursday: spell words orally, take practice test; Write basic sentences using the vocabulary words and let student add descriptive words.

Friday: Review, take the spelling test.

Math Reinforcement/Science Activities and Experiments/Geography/History/ Art/Music/Drama

Monday: Read through the section on the brain and nervous system and make your plan of study. Some suggestions for deeper investigation might be: effects of stroke, work of a physical therapist or neuropsychologist, understanding how pathways are formed when learning new tasks, epilepsy, cerebral palsy, Alzheimer disease, growth problems in children, or spinal cord injuries. Diagram the brain parts and learn the function of the cerebrum and cerebellum. What is left brain right brain dominance? What part of the brain deals with memory? Try short term memory games (see Science Activities and Experiments: 4-8). What are the effects of drugs and alcohol on memory. Choose one of the art projects, like using different color clay to make a model of the brain. Tell what you have learned about the cerebellum and its function.

Tuesday: Locate the thalamus, hypothalamus, pituitary gland, and the brain stem. Learn about what activities they control. Chart the different areal of your brain that control your actions (Science Activities and Experiments: 9-12). What causes you to grow, and mature? Hormones! The Pituitary gland controlled by the hypo-thalamus release the hormones that allow this to happen. The brain stem is the control center for involuntary actions (like breathing, heart beat, and other organ functions). Discuss and read your resource books concerning these parts of the brain. Have your student hold his breath as at a point they will not be able to control not taking a breath. Play some memory games. Continue to work on reports or research projects.

Wednesday: Spinal Cord and nerves are the body's messaging system. Study the Braille system. How does this relate to the nervous system? (Science Activities and Experiments: 9-12) What are nerves and neurons? How do nerves help in the learning of new tasks. Check your students reaction time (Science Activities and Experiments K-3). Many brain and spinal cord injuries occur during car accidents and during sports or recreational activities. How can we protect our brain? Continue to spend time researching your topic.

Thursday: Test your child's memory by giving another blank diagram of the brain and see if your students can name all the parts. Choose further experiments from your resource book like Blood and Guts or Janice Van Cleave's Human Body for Every Kid and Janice Van Cleave's Biology for Every Kid. Continue to compile your research on your topic of special interest. Plan how you can best share your information.

Friday: Wrap up the week with reports, oral presentations, summaries of experiments, and memory games.

Lesson Plans Grades 4-8 Week 6

Bible/ Religion Studies-Gen. 1: 26, Gen. 1:28, Ps. 139:14 Teacher's choice of verses and lessons

Morning warm up: 5 minute write up! A few quick ideas— but let YOUR imagination go and think of some of your own starters: truth, falsehood, embryo, baby, evolution, creation, male, female.

Teaching Outline-Monday-Evolution Creation debate **Tuesday**– Human Reproduction **Wednesday**– Genetics **Thursday**– DNA **Friday**– reports and presentations

Reading—Every day: Reading 30 minutes to one hour everyday both silently and aloud. Check comprehension/ review note cards of research for book reports or oral reports.

Language Arts, Spelling, Vocabulary—

Monday: assign words and writing definitions on index cards, write each word 5 times.

Tuesday: use the words in a sentence, write words 5 times each.

Wednesday: write words 5 times each alphabetize the words; write the harder words several in row with only one spelled correctly and see if student can pick out the correct spelling. Select a paragraph for dictation and sentence diagraming.

Thursday: spell words orally, take practice test; Write basic sentences using the vocabulary words and let student add descriptive words.

Friday: Review, take the spelling test.

Math Reinforcement/Science Activities and Experiments/Geography/History/ Art/Music/Drama-

Monday: Read through the section on Reproduction. We have chosen to begin our study at the stage of union of egg and sperm and the beginning of a new single-cell person. It is the parent's prerogative as to what additional information the student is ready to learn. We begin with flaws of evolutionary thinking that demonstrate that evolution being taught as fact is really only a theory not proven science and with serious defects. Do some research on Charles Darwin and what he theorized.

Take time if you have not studied this debate before to cover it. For example, one of the many flaws in evolutionary theory is the absence of transitional fossils. Give your students the tools and understanding to point out the flaws of evolution when they are challenged by friends from the public school. Check out resources from our reading list and check out: http://www.tccsa.tc/articles/ (Twin Cities Creation Science Association) for an awesome book list. Science in Creation Week by David Unfred has some hands on experiments.

Tuesday: Human reproduction beginning with the development of the human fetus (which means little one) trace it's development from fertilization through the first year after birth. Make some drawings of the path a fertilized egg takes and it's development. Refer to your reference books like Steve Parker's The Human Body Book reading the sections on human embryonic development.

Wednesday: Read about genes and heredity. Look up the Scientist, Fr. Gregor Johann Mendel, and the work on genetics. See if you can make a model (chart) showing how traits are passed on to offspring. What is DNA? What does it stand for and how is it related to the work of Mendel. Write a short report on this scientists contributions. Mendel was an "Austrian monk," but actually he was born in what is now called the Czech Republic. Look at the map and do a "side bar" article about the map of Europe in 1822 and the Austro-Hungarian Empire.

Thursday: Continue the research started yesterday on DNA, chromosomes, and genes. Study the work of Sir Francis Crick, who discovered DNA. (Science Activities and Experiments: 9-12) What is the Genome Project? Construct a Lego DNA molecule. (Science Activities and Experiments:4-8) Read through the section on DNA and research something that captures your curiosity. Takes notes and plan an oral presentation for Friday.

Friday: Review the weeks findings and make presentations, go over research and discuss/debate the creation/evolution theories.

Lesson Plans Grades 4-8 Week 7

Bible/ Religion Studies— Psalms 33:18, Psalms 119:103, Proverbs 1:8, Phil 4:18, Mark 5:28, Gen 11:19 or Teacher's choice.

Morning warm up: 5 minute write up! A few quick ideas— but let YOUR imagination go and think of some of your own starters: blindness , deafness, sign language, sensitivity, babble, stinky.

Teaching Outline-Monday-5 senses **Tuesday–** 5 senses **Wednesday–** Language **Thursday–** Language **Friday–** reports and presentations

Reading—Every day: Reading 30 minutes to one hour everyday both silently and aloud. Check comprehension/ review note cards of research for book reports or oral reports.

Language Arts, Spelling, Vocabulary—

Monday: assign words and writing definitions on index cards, write each word 5 times.

Tuesday: use the words in a sentence, write words 5 times each; Describing a sunset if you were color blind. (Language Arts Ideas 4-8)

Wednesday: write words 5 times each alphabetize the words; write the harder words several in row with only one spelled correctly and see if student can pick out the correct spelling. Select a paragraph for dictation and sentence for diagraming.

Thursday: spell words orally, take practice test; Write basic sentences using the vocabulary words and let student add descriptive words.

Friday: Review, take the spelling test.

Math Reinforcement/Science Activities and Experiments/Geography/History/ Art/Music/Drama-

Monday: Read through the section on the senses. Print out diagrams of eyes, ear, tongue, nose and skin. (kidshealth.org) or make your own. Have students label them. Let students choose one or two senses to become "experts" on and begin doing research. Decide how this research will be presented on Friday. Consider doing research on sign language or learning braille especially if you have studied the senses in the past and they know the parts of and function already.

Look deeper into the uniqueness of human language and how complex our communications really are compared to animals ability to communicate. Decide now what mode of reporting your learning will take on Friday.

Using your resources have the students read about eyes and sight, ears and hearing and mouth and taste. Check your resource books for experiments and possible activities for these senses.

Tuesday: Using resources read about the nose and smelling, and skin and touch. Check these books for experiments and possible activities for these senses. Don't forget to make diagrams and label them. Do the experiment about melanin (Science Activities and Experiments:4-8). Observe dead skin cells with a magnifying glass (Science Activities and Experiments:4-8). Do the experiment to see if you are waterproof (Science Activities and Experiments:4-8). Study the art of fingerprinting (Geography and History Ideas 4-8). Make thumbprint art (Art/Music K-3). Measure the surface area of the skin of your body. Devise different ways to do this (Math reinforcement Ideas 4–8). How were the bodies of ancient Egyptian mummies prepared for burial? Why did this treatment preserve the skin? (Geography and History Ideas 4-8)

Wednesday: Read from the Teaching Outline about Language, don't forget to read the account in the Bible, Gen. 11: 19. Research the origin of languages. Using a blank world map, chart the locations of the different languages (Geography/History Ideas 4-8. Learn some basic phrases in another language. Recall what part of the brain contains the language functions. Research how victims of strokes go about relearning speech.

Thursday: Make a chart of different consonant sound (Science Activities and Experiments; 4-8). Prepare your presentation of what you have learned this week. Make Trivia cards for your Trivia Game so that you can play it on Friday with your family.

Friday: Give oral reports, demonstration of experiments, projects that were done this week. Play your Trivia Game.

Lesson Plans Grades 4-8 Week 8

Bible/ Religion Studies— Teacher's choice.

Morning warm up: 5 minute write up! A few quick ideas— but let YOUR imagination go and think of some of your own starters: pigment, dignity, racism, fairness, population, inventions, prejudice, technology, intelligence.

Teaching Outline-Monday-Race **Tuesday**– Human History **Wednesday**– Technology **Thursday**– Review and preparation of papers/ projects **Friday**– reports and presentations.

Reading—Every day: Reading 30 minutes to one hour everyday both silently and aloud. Check comprehension/ review note cards of research for book reports or oral reports

Language Arts, Spelling, Vocabulary—

Monday: assign words and writing definitions on index cards, write each word 5 times.

Tuesday: use the words in a sentence, write words 5 times each; Take five or six sentences from a book you are reading and answer the five "W's."(Language Arts Ideas 4-8).

Wednesday: write words 5 times each alphabetize the words; write the harder words several in row with only one spelled correctly and see if student can pick out the correct spelling. Select a paragraph for dictation and sentence for diagraming.

Thursday: spell words orally, take practice test; Write basic sentences using the vocabulary words and let student add descriptive words.

Friday: Review, take the spelling test.

Math Reinforcement/Science Activities and Experiments/Geography/History/ Art/Music/Drama-

Monday: Read through the section on the Races. What skin types have a higher concentration of melanin? Check out your resources, Of Pandas and People, and research the influence evolution has had on the equality of the races. Do some research on Racial Prejudices and write a paper on the damage this type of thinking has caused in society and in our world. Research the way propaganda is used by those in power and especially the way words can be used to dehumanize a group of people. Compare words that dehumanized the Jews in Nazi Germany to how Pro Abortion groups describe the pre-born child. What form of reporting are you going to use in demonstrating your learning? Posters and visuals might be useful.

Tuesday: Read the section on Human History about population. Do the suggested map exercise locating the populations that are starving and research the largest populations locating and labeling them on you world map (Geography/History: 4-8) Do some research on the overpopulation claims and on the claims of those who say the earth is not overpopulated. (Geography/History Ideas: 4-8) What are your opinions?

Wednesday: Today look at the inventions throughout human history. Choose an invention to research (Geography/History: 4-8). Sometimes people today think they are more intelligent than those who lived earlier in history. Do you believe this? Look at the types of things that students were required to learn in early America, or in the ancient world of the Greek or the Egyptians. Do you know these facts?

Thursday: Choose one of the areas you have been researching this week to put more effort into today and add more information and decide how you will present your learning on Friday. Choose a method that will showcase your topic.

Friday: Make a summary report of this weeks learning and make your final report/ presentation. And now take a look back over the information, exercises, experiments, and activities you have been doing this last 8 weeks and marvel at all you have accomplished and learned. What is one area or topic that you hav learned the most? Celebrate the gift of life.

Reading List
4-8

*Books may be difficult to find in the library and some are no longer in print but you can find them on Amazon or eBay fairly easily and for great prices.

Oral or Silent Reading:
(Depending on child's reading ability)

Exploring the History of Medicine, by John Hudson Tiner, New Leaf Publishing Group, 1999.

Galen and the Gateway to Medicine, by Jeanne Bendick, Introduction by Benjamin D. Wiker Bethlehem Books, 2002.

Gregor Mendel: And the Roots of Genetics, by Edward Edelson, Oxford University Press, 1999.

Gregor Mendel: Genetics Pioneer, by Lynn Van Gorp, Teacher Created Materials Publishing, Huntington Beach, CA, 2008

Helen Keller: Toward the Light by Stewart and Polly Anne Graff
Publisher: Dell, 1992, 80 pp.
This book deals with the life of Helen Keller and is one of the better books I have seen. There are many books about her life yet this one tells it in a simplified manner dealing with her life as an adult.

*Johannes Kepler: Giant of Faith and Science
Publisher: Mott Media, 1999, 207 pp.
This book is written from a Christian perspective and tells about the discoveries, struggles, and triumphs of Kepler's life.

*Origin of Life Evolution/Creation by Richard B. Bliss, Gary E. Parker, and Duane T. Gish
Publisher: C.L.P. Publishers, 1990, 76 pp.
A scientific model of Creation and evolution explaining the origins of life with an emphasis on presenting data and allowing the reader to make a choice as to which makes the most sense.

Soldier Doctor by Clara Ingram Judson
Publisher: Scribner, 1942, 151 pp.
This book is about a man who was an army doctor and would one day become the U.S. Surgeon General. He was determined to find the cure for yellow fever, which was at that time one of the most horrible diseases. This is

A great read aloud book for the family about one man's determination to prove his theory.

The Greatest Doctor of Ancient Times: Hippocrates and His Oath, by Mary
  Gow, Berkley Heights, NJ: Enslow Publishers, 2010.

Unlocking the Mysteries of Creation by Dennis R. Petersen
  Publisher: Bridge-Logos Publishers, 2008, 2012, 240 pp.
  This book explains the complexity of the living cell in a manner that is forthright and clear. Have your child read the sections on the cells, early civilizations, technology, (actually the whole book is a wonderful addition to your home library).

Why Do Our Bodies Stop Growing? by Dr. P. Witfield & Dr. R. Witfield
  Publisher: Viking Juvenile, 1988, 96 pp.
  This book is written in a question and answer format that answers questions such as whether skin is alive, how cuts heal, what a heart attack is, why we breathe, what a liver is for, etc. It is colorful and written in a way that will hold a student's interest.

Activity and Experiment
Resource List
4-8

*Books may be difficult to find in the library and some are no longer in print but you can find them on Amazon or eBay fairly easily and for great prices.

A+ Projects in Chemistry by Janice VanCleave
> Publisher: John Wiley & Sons, Inc., 1993, 240 pp.
> Great experiments on biochemistry, vitamins, minerals, proteins, etc. Most experiments use easy -to-find items with a minimum of preparation. Some of the experiments may be difficult for younger children.

Biology for Every Kid by Janice VanCleave
> Publisher: John Wiley & Sons, Inc., 1990, 240 pp.
> 101 experiments, approximately thirty-five of which deal with the body. I enjoy these books because they do experiments using the scientific method. This a great book to give older children and allow them to do experimentation on their own.

Blood and Guts by Linda Allison
> Publisher: Little, Brown and Company, 1976, pp. 127 pp.
> (Complete review Resource List for K-3) You may want to give this book to grades 5 and up to do experiments on their own. (Don't for- get a copy of the Scientific Method Sheet)

How the Body Works by Steve Parker
> Publisher: Dorling Kindersley Publishers Ltd, 1999, 192 pp.
> (See complete review Resource List for K-3.) There are many activities that require building so now is the time to get Dad involved!

Human Anatomy Coloring Book by Margaret Matt, Text by Joe Ziemian
> Publisher: Dover Coloring Book, 1982, 48 pp.
> If you are like me and prefer coloring to dissection, this book is for you! It includes the systems of the body and much more. The finely detailed drawings are perfect for the middle years. The text is a bit technical, so added explanations will probably be needed in the younger grades. I highly recommend this book!

Janice VanCleave's The Human Body for Every Kid: Easy Activities that
> Makes Learning Fun, by Janice Van Cleave, New York, New York: J Wiley, C 1995.

Science in the Creation Week: Content & Hands On Science Skills Curriculum Grades 2-5, by David Unfred, Nobel Publishing Associates, 1995.

The Body Book: Easy to Make Models that Teach, by Donald M. Silver and Patricia J. Wynne Scholastic , Inc. 1999, 2008.

700 Science Experiments for Everyone by Unesco
Publisher: Doubleday Books, 1964, 256 pp.
Originally printed in 1956 for science teachers in devastated countries, this revised book contains hundreds of great science experiments that tie in with almost any topic you are teaching. Sure enough, under the section relating to the body there are great experiments, and under "light" are some that deal with the eyes. I use this book often.

*The Franklin Institute Resources for science learning (Internet Site)
C 1996-2010 the Franklin Institute web team@www.fi.edu

Vocabulary/Spelling List
4-8

This list is to be used as a *basis* for your vocabulary and spelling words for this unit study. Look at the list of words given for grades K-3. If there are any words that your child does not know, add them to the list below. If you feel some words are too difficult, exclude them. If the child does not know the meaning of the words, have him look them up in a dictionary, science dictionary, or encyclopedia and write a brief definition. Add to, subtract from, or customize this list to make it your own.

adenoids	dendrite	mandible	quadriceps
aorta	dentine	maxilla	rectum
appendix	dermis	medulla	retina
atrium (right & left)	duct	melanin	root canal
auditory bones	enzyme	membrane	scapula
auditory nerves	epidermis	meninges	scar tissue
axon	epiglottis	metatarsals	sclera
biceps	Eustachian tube	midbrain	semicircular canals
bile ducts	glands	nerve fibers	spleen
bronchus	hair follicle	nucleus	sweat gland duct
capillary	heredity	nutrient	tarsals
cell body	larynx	optic nerve	tendon
cerebellum	ligaments	ossify	thyroid
cerebrum	lumbar	pain receptor	tibia
cilia	lymph	palate	trachea
cochlea	lymph system	perspiration	triceps
colon	femur	phalanges	tympanic membranes
connective tissue	fibula	pharynx	vena cava (superior & inferior)
cornea	fontanelles	photoreceptors	
cranium	ganglia	platelets	ventricle (right & left)
deltoid	gingival	pulmonary artery	voluntary muscles
		pulmonary vein	

Spelling/ Vocabulary and Grammar Ideas
4-8

Use vocabulary and spelling words interchangeably in the following activities. Choose the words you want your child to learn to spell.

◊ Use the words in sentences showing their meaning. Use the sentences the child has written to study the parts of speech. Continue the list below with any of the parts of speech you are currently studying. For example:

   Underline a noun once

   Underline a verb twice

   Put a squiggly line under an adjective

   Put two squiggly lines under an adverb

   Put a box around a preposition

   Circle a pronoun with a "P" above it

   Highlight direct and indirect objects

   Put parenthesis around prepositional phrases and arrows to what they modify.

◊ Use colored pencils or markers for the grammar activity, assigning a color to each of the parts of speech.

◊ Have your children use pictures to remind them of what the words mean. They can draw or cut pictures out of a magazine or paper. Have them keep a vocabulary book as a reference. Use loose leaf papers and a spiral ring binder so that you can add to it easily.

◊ Have the children make vocabulary cards. Use index cards: on one side write the word, on the back side the definition. Use the words in different games.

◊ Use the vocabulary words to play "hopscotch." Take chalk and draw a hopscotch grid outdoors (or make one indoors by marking out large squares with colored yarn). Lay one vocabulary card, word side up, on each square. Play hopscotch. In order to keep the card, the child must give the correct definition of the word in the square in which he lands. Continue to put more cards in the spaces as they are used up. When all the cards have been used, the child with the most cards wins.

◊ Give each letter of the alphabet a secret code. Have each of the children write several difficult vocabulary words (ones they may be having trouble with) in secret code. Have them put all the words on scraps of paper. Put them in a bag and pull them out randomly. Try to decipher the words. (Have your children make up their own secret code.)

◊ Have your children make a crossword puzzle using the vocabulary words. They can make easy word searches (or puzzles) for younger brothers or sisters.

◊ Write the vocabulary words several times (three or four) in a row; misspell all but one of them. Have your child circle the words that are spelled correctly.

◊ Take index cards, cut them in half and on one piece of the card write the vocabulary words (those difficult to learn). On the other piece write the definition. Put all of them in a paper bag. Randomly remove five cards each (if you are playing with someone else). See if you have any matches (use a glossary list to check the definitions if you don't know them). Ask the other person if he has the definition for one of your words, or the word for one of your definitions. If he answers no, take a card from the bag. The person with the most matches wins.

◊ Use the vocabulary words in basic sentences and have the children change them by making the sentence more descriptive, specific or interesting. For example: *He has biceps.* Changed to: *His biceps bulged under the strain of lifting the logs.*

◊ Study the Greek and Latin origins of words. For example, "kinesis" means movement. (*English from the Roots Up*)

Language Arts Ideas

4-8

◊ Use the Scripture 1 Cor. 12:12-27 as a basis for an oral presentation on the human body and the way its systems are interdependent.

◊ Begin an open-ended story and take turns adding to the story orally in a group. (This is especially fun with a group of different-aged children). For example: "It had always been my dream to be on a space mission, but never did I imagine the "space" in which I would travel. As I checked the instrument panel which contained a computer display, I still couldn't believe I had actually been chosen from thousands of students. There were two students and six adults on board; my job was to monitor the computer screen which, for the moment, was showing a myriad of signals I had never before seen. It worked automatically, taking pictures as our space ship hurtled through the blood stream of a human body!" (This can also be used as a written assignment.) Variation: Concentrate on parts of the body you are studying: lungs, heart, etc. Change mission of the trip or characterization.

◊ Use a paragraph from one of the books you are reading on anatomy to give dictation. Check for proper spelling and punctuation.

◊ Research the difference between M.D. (Medical Doctor) and D.O. (Doctor Osteopath). In what ways are they similar? In what major ways are they different?

◊ Write different types of poems about the Creation of man.

◊ Study the origin of the names of the different parts of the body. Write a comparison of the original meaning of the words and the commonly "accepted" meaning of the words today.

◊ Read several books on anatomy. Choose different chapters of the books to check for comprehension by using any of the following ideas: identify the main idea, give the book a better title, infer beyond what is specifically stated, identify the correct sequence of events, identify facts and fiction, identify facts and opinions, briefly outline the book.

◊ Take five or six sentences from a book you are reading and answer the five "W's". Take a sheet of paper and make five headings, labeling them who, what, where, why, and when. Take each sentence and answer those questions by writing a portion of the sentence under the specific topic heading.

◊ Write a paragraph or more discussing why you do or do not agree with the scientists' (evolutionists') findings about evolution. For example, what are the facts that point to evolution (if any)? What do Creationists and evolutionists have to say about it?

◊ Divide a sheet of paper into two columns. Label the headings Facts vs. Opinions. Under the two headings, list as much data as you can find to support evolution, and compare this to what the Bible has to say about the beginning of mankind.

◊ Find articles in the newspaper or magazines that deal with anatomy- related topics. Ask questions about each article when you have finished reading it. If the article contains material contrary to Creationists' viewpoint, consider writing a letter to the editor using a well-researched article with quotes from various scientists to substantiate your point. Check punctuation and grammar! Submit your age and perhaps the fact that you are homeschooled when responding to the article.

◊ Research contagious (or infectious) diseases. What effect have antibiotics had on health? Who made discoveries in this field? Read a biography about a scientist who made great strides in the area of medicine, such as Louis Pasteur.

◊ Research ways to fight illness without medicine. What are ways to fight a cold without taking medicine? What are the benefits of not taking   medication? What are the benefits of taking medicine? Have a debate with another person, each taking one position. Use facts to support your claims.

◊ Read *Soldier Doctor* by Clara Judson. How does this doctor struggle to prove a theory that he has about the spread of a deadly disease? Write a sequel to this story. Write a fictitious account of someone's life that was affected by his findings.

◊ Write a one-act play about the above account, or use another book you have read (such as *Helen Keller)*. How does your character change? Is it due to the advances of medicine, another's determination, or by the grace of God?

◊ Write a short story from a bit of food's perspective as it goes from being eaten through the digestive process. Talk about things from a *scientific* perspective. What juices, muscles, enzymes, etc. are being used to break down the food?

◊ Write a short story entitled *"A Day in the Life of a Blood Cell"*. What are its functions; where does it travel? Does it have a close call, perhaps because it has been injured? Be as creative and realistic as possible!

◊ What is a phantom limb? (See teaching outline.) Do an interview of a fictional person who has lost his limb (leg or arm) in an accident. How does he feel? Why should he have hope?

◊ What would it be like if we saw everything in black and white? Describe a bouquet of colors, a sunset, another person. Use as many adjectives and colors as you can.

◊ What is the traditional significance of colors? (See teaching outline.) How have these changed or stayed the same through the years? What did people wear years ago, after the death of a dear one? Has this changed? In what countries is this still prevalent?

◊ Research one or more of the systems of the body. How does this system contribute to the overall well-being of the body? Does this system perform a necessary function? Why? What would happen if it did not exist?

◊ What parts of the body are unnecessary for life? List them. What labels are placed on people who do not have one or more functioning items on the list? For example, a person with eyes that do not see would be called blind (or visually impaired).

◊ What devices have been invented to improve our "quality" of life? For example, those who have difficulty seeing clearly can wear prescription glasses, etc.

Math Reinforcement Ideas
4-8

◊ What are some mathematical facts relating the "price" of the contents of our body? What do scientists say the mineral content is worth? What about the molecular content? Write word problems based on your findings. (See Teaching Outline.)

◊ What is your reaction time? (The time it takes for your brain to process instructions relating to an action your body must perform.) Do this activity with a friend. How quickly can you catch a ruler (or any object) another person drops in front of you? The faster you react, the less time the ruler has to fall. Where will your hand be on the ruler? At the top, in the middle, or at the lower end? Record your findings in centimeters: the top of the ruler (30 cm.), the middle (15 cm.), or the end (1 cm.). Can this reaction time improve with practice? Do this ten times and chart and graph your results. Convert your findings to mm.

◊ How many times do you breathe in and out in one day? An average adult inhales then exhales about .5L (about 1 pint) of air per breath and has a respiration rate of about 12-20 breaths per minute. Figure out how much air is breathed in one day. (Answer: 500 ft^3 and 14,000,000 ft^3 of air in a lifetime! *You and Your Body*) Count the number of times you breathe in and out in thirty seconds, multiply the amount by two. How many breaths do you take in one day? Why don't all the people and animals in the world use up the oxygen? (Research photosynthesis.)

◊ Research the names and proportions of the gasses in the air we breathe. (Air consists of 78% nitrogen, 21% oxygen, and 1% other gasses: argon, carbon dioxide, hydrogen, krypton, neon, helium, and xenon.) Make a circle graph to show your findings. (*You and Your Body*)

◊ Measure the surface area of skin of your body. Devise different ways to do this. Use the metric system.

◊ Prepare the following cleanliness survey and chart the results. Ask five or more people to complete the survey. Answer yes or no and give a point value to each. An example of questions and points are listed. Change or add to the following list. I brush my teeth every day. (5 points) I brush my teeth after every meal. (10 points) I floss my teeth every day. (10 points) I brush my teeth after every snack. (15 points) Take the results for each person and add them up. What was the average score of five people? Variation: Do this with hand washing.

◊ Calculate calories (or fat grams) of meals eaten in one day. Use a calorie book or the labels of food eaten to do this. Chart your results. Research how many calories (or fat grams) are necessary for your age. Take into account your body size, including height.

◊ Research the number of bones in the bodies of different aged people. How do the number of bones in the body differ from an infant to a child to an adult? How many bones are in the skull, spine and rib cage?

◊ Measure the amount of food you eat in one day. Use metric (a scale with grams listed will be helpful). Do this for a few days (or a week). What is the total average weight of food you ate per day? Multiply this number by the number of days in a week, month, or year. Research how much scientists say people eat. How does your number compare? Were you close?

◊ Research body temperatures and the effects of extreme cold on the body. What temperature can your hands and feet withstand before being frostbitten? What temperature can the core of your body withstand? Why is there such an extreme difference in the temperature different parts of the body can withstand? What can you do in the case of an emergency?

◊ How strong are you? Use a bathroom scale and record which part of your body (muscles) is the most powerful. Try pushing on the scale with your hands, in between your legs, and whatever other way you can devise to register pounds. Convert your answers to metric.

Science Activities and Experiments
4-8

A good understanding of the scientific method is a must at this grade level. (Felice's personal bias!) For an overview of the scientific method see page 4) Remember to formulate your question and hypothesis before you begin the experiment. At this age give the children flexibility to experiment. If they have an idea of something they want to try, give them the time to do it. It is helpful if they write out their procedures using the scientific method sheets (include in this book). In the event that they discover something amazing, they will be able to duplicate the experiment. *Always use caution when doing any science projects and experiments. Parental supervision necessary! Remember: Whenever using raw meat wash hands and the surrounding areas with anti-bacterial soap!*

◊ What process does oxygen go through after it is inhaled and passes through the cells, organs, and is carried to the lungs and exhaled? (See Teaching Outline.)

◊ Compare the blood, as it is necessary for our life, and how Christ saved us by His Blood. Use the *Bible* to back up your claim.

◊ Make up body "trivia cards". Use the teaching outline for information and other resources. Ask questions such as, "How many round trips does a blood cell make through the circulatory system?"

◊ Make a model of the arm. Take two pieces of poster board. Measure your arm: (1) from the elbow to your wrist, and (2) from your shoulder to your elbow. For number (1) cut into an oblong shape squaring off the edges, for number

(2) cut into an oblong shape, but round off both edges. Connect the joint with a brad clip. Attach rubber bands with brads (experiment to see if you can make it work) to the elbow side of your model. Now attach string with brads to the forearm to make your model move. How difficult is this? How much awe should we have of God who made us so wonderfully? (You can do the above project with wood. *How the Body Works*)

◊ Make models of your head and neck, or leg and foot with cardboard, paper towel rolls, or wood. Can you devise ways to make them move?

◊ Put your hand over one eye and leave the other open. Walk outside or sit in a brightly lit room. After several minutes (experiment with different times) look at both eyes closely in the mirror. What do you observe? How does more time make a difference to the pupil of your eyes?

◊ What are optical illusions? Try this one. Take a sheet of paper and roll it into a long tube. Tape this to keep it from unrolling. Hold the tube up to your right eye leaving both eyes opened. Look at an object across the room and place your left hand against the tube with your palm facing towards you. What do you see? Why does this happen? How can you alter the effect? (*Biology for Every Kid)*

◊ Does your skin color change? Put a bandage on one finger. Leave it on for several days. Remove the bandage and observe the color of your finger. How does it look? Why is some of the skin lighter? What skin types have a higher concentration of melanin?

◊ Demonstrate osmosis of a cell membrane (a semi-permeable barrier). Put two tablespoons of cornstarch into a small sandwich baggie and mix it with water until the bag will sink in a small beaker of water. Put a twistie tie on the baggie and place it into a beaker making sure it is above the water level (so that water won't seep in). Add a few drops of iodine to the water turning it a pale brownish color. Leave overnight. Observe the effects on the cornstarch mixture. Why did this happen? Why didn't the water change color? How could evolution explain the complexity of cells to allow certain molecules, such as water, free passage through the cell membrane, while other substances, such as proteins, can only pass through at certain sites?(*How the Body Works*)

◊ Observe dead skin cells with a magnifying glass (or microscope). Place ink on the back of your hand and let it dry. Using a piece of tape place it over the inked area, peel it off and place it (sticky side down) on a slide. Observe it with a magnifying glass or microscope.

◊ Are you waterproof? Find out! Take a few drops of dish soap and put it in a container with a half cup of water. Rub the palm of your right hand with alcohol, then use a straw or dropper and put several drops of soapy water on your right hand. Have someone else put several drops on your left hand. Compare the two. What happened? What is the sebum layer? Why does our skin wrinkle after long baths or swimming?

◊ Do dissections. Use the book *Blood and Guts* for information and ideas, or dissect raw chicken pieces. Note the way the muscles (meat) and cartilage adhere to the bones.

◊ Use a large can of vegetables and place it in one hand. Squeeze and release the

129

can and feel the tendons in your arm with your other hand. While holding the can, bend your elbow, lift your forearm, and twist it all the while noting which muscles are being used to do these activities. You should be able to feel your tendons, biceps, deltoids, and trapezius muscles.

◊ How long does it take for your muscles to tire? Do sit-ups slowly, feeling the muscles in your abdomen. Now do as many sit-ups as you can until you can't do anymore. Do this over a several week period. What happens to your muscles? Devise an exercise plan to do daily (or every other day). Why is exercise important to health? How does exercise effect your sleeping, eating habits, or weight?

◊ Take your pulse after different exercises. Which ones cause your heart to beat the fastest? What is happening to your body as your heartbeat accelerates?

◊ Wrap cotton around a thermometer and a plastic tube (or use a straw) making sure the ends are sticking out and place into a glass jar. Make sure that the thermometer is held securely and that you can read the temperature. Place one end of the tube in your mouth and breathe in deeply. Then breathe out away from the tube. Do this ten times and read the temperature. Now breathe in from the air and out through the tube ten times. What is the temperature? Is this different? Why?

◊ Use a pinwheel and devise an experiment to use wind power as a force.

◊ What foods give you the most energy? Fill an empty soft drink can with water and place a thermometer in it. Note the temperature. Place this on a cake rack.

Hold a peanut (uncooked) with tongs over a candle until it catches fire. Place this on a foil covered tile and slide it under the cake rack to heat the water in the can. Check the temperature from time to time. How hot does the water get? (*How the Body Works*)

◊ What is DNA? Use tinker toy blocks or other structures to make a DNA molecule. How complex is it?

◊ Make a chart of different consonant sounds. Pay particular attention to where the tongue is placed in making these sounds. What are voiced consonants?

◊ Study the brain. What part of the brain deals with memory? Try various short term memory games. Write a set of numbers, for example, 45, 60, 20. Say them to another person, have them say the numbers back. Continue to add numbers to the sequence until the person can no longer remember them correctly. Variation: use names, colors, or places.

◊ What is long term memory? What part of the brain deals with memories? What are the effects of exposure to drugs and alcohol on memory?

Geography and History Ideas
4-8

◊ Study early scientists. Choose one scientist and learn as much as possible about him. What drove him to find a cure (make a discovery etc.)? Pretend you are his apprentice. What did you find or discover? What was it like living in the _____ century? What was the favorite food, activity, or musician of the day?

◊ Study some early remedies in medicine. What were some that actually worked? Which remedies were dangerous to the health of the person? What were the practices of quarantine? How did the practices change through the centuries?

◊ Map out the places where scientists who made discoveries in the field of anatomy lived (see teaching outline). Where was the most concentrated number of scientists found? Why?

◊ What obstacles did early scientists encounter? Were people willing to believe all of their claims? Why or why not? How were some of these scientists paid to continue their research?

◊ How were the bodies of ancient Egyptian mummies prepared for burial? Why did this treatment preserve the skin? Would the body have lasted as long if it had not been treated? Why? Did other cultures practice this way of body preservation? Why did the Egyptians do this?

◊ How did food and living conditions affect the body in relation to height? In relation to life span? At what time in recorded history were poor living conditions at their worse? Where could you go to look up this information?

◊ Study the art of fingerprinting. How did this practice begin? When was it discovered to be an effective means of identification? What is the latest trend in identification (eyes)? What steps are being taken in various forms of identification?

◊ What was happening in other places of the world when yellow fever was incurable? Chart the happenings throughout history by making a time line beginning with ancient scientists.

◊ What does the Bible say about diseases? Cleanliness? What books of the Bible first dealt with the washing of hands before meals? List the places in Scripture that refer to cleanliness.

◊ Use a globe or atlas to find countries where outbreaks of diseases are still prevalent. Listen to the news or read the paper and keep a record of outbreaks. Note your source, date, and geographical location. Research the people and their lifestyle. What effect does culture have on cures? How much does politics affect the health of a nation?

◊ Using a map, locate populations that are starving. What is being done to help the people? How much does government intervention determine a relief effort's success?

◊ Using a blank world map, chart the locations of the different languages. Instead of writing the name of the country, for example, for France, write French. Use the most prevalent language excluding dialects.

◊ How have inventions changed history? Take one invention and research it. Answer the following questions: Where was the inventor born? How well received was the invention? How much trouble did the inventor have in making his invention? Was it something that radically changed the way we live, or did it take years and many improvements before change was noticeable?

◊ Research the origins of languages and use a map to label the spread of humanity. Where was the biggest concentration of inhabitants for years?

◊ Research the largest populations and, using a world map, label countries by their populations. How is population explosion a myth? What information can you find to answer the following questions: What state in the U.S. could hold the *entire population* of the world? How much room would this give each person? How much room would these people have for recreation, food, travel, etc.? (Human Life International)

Art and Music Ideas
4-8

Art

◊ Have the children write vocabulary words in the shape of their definition. For example, the word "biceps" would be drawn in the shape of a bulging muscle, "perspiration" could be drawn in the shapes of drops of water, etc.

◊ Make a "body" out of spare parts, recyclables, or left over sewing material. Be creative. For example, use a two-liter bottle for the torso; sticks for the legs and arms held together with clay; a balloon for the head, buttons for the eyes, nose, and mouth; paper for the ears; yarn for the hair, etc. Make a family from recyclables!

◊ Draw different body organs. Label them.

◊ Make a wire sculpture of the body using florist wire. Bend the wire to make the body and use clay as the base.

◊ Use different color clay as a medium for making a body, portrait, or organ of the body. Use poster board or colored construction paper as the base. Draw a light outline in pencil. Roll different colors of clay into a ball or cylinder. Press onto the paper and blend the colors together to form your picture. For example, once you have a base using a light (or dark) color for the face, you can use blue (or whatever color) for the eyes, brown for the hair etc. This makes a great picture!

Music

◊ Study different wind instruments. Talk about what musicians must do to maintain their instruments. How does lip placement and technique affect performance? What parts of instruments must be cleaned regularly because of saliva collecting in them?

◊ Sing! Notice the work of your diaphragm, lungs, etc.

◊ What is pitch? Listen to songs and chart the different pitch levels. If your stereo has a system that allows you to adjust levels to alter the sounds, add more base and treble. Subtract some, how do the adjustments alter the sound?

◊ Try making a drum. Stretch a balloon over a surface such as a tin can with one or both ends cut out. Experiment with different sizes of cans. How does the sound change? What happens when you hit the stretched surface with different objects?

◊ Describe the difference between a sonata, sonatina, minuet, and a symphony.

Creation Anatomy
Grades 9-12

Objective: To study anatomy from a Biblical perspective through observation, comparison, research, and experiments.

Topics of Study:

Outline

I. Body Analogy
 A. Scripture
 B. Value Human Body
 C. Price Paid

II. Circulatory System and Respiration
 A. Scriptures
 B. Terminology
 C. Function
 D. Heart — Arteries and Veins
 E. Blood Components
    1. Cells
    2. Shape
    3. Function
    F. Respiration

III. Injuries and Healing
 A. Components of Blood
    1. Plasma
    2. Nutrients and Minerals
    3. Leukocytes (white cells)
    4. Granulocytes
    5. Thrombocytes
    6. Platelets
    7. Fibrinogen, Antigen, Lymphocytes, Antibodies
 B. Immunity
    1. Response to infections
    2. Creating antibodies
    3. Lymph System
    4. Science catches up with the Bible

IV. Skeletal System and Muscles
A. Composition of framework
B. Function of framework
C. Muscles
      1. Function
      2. Types
D. Joints, Ligaments, Tendons
E. The hand

V. Digestive System
A. Organs
B. Fluids
C. Functions

VI. Nervous System and Brain

VII. Reproductive System

VIII. DNA

IX. Senses
A. Auditory
B. Vision
C. Olfactory and Taste
D. Tactile and Skin

X. Language

XI. Races

XII. Human History

Anatomy: A Two Months Study At A Glance
Grades 9-12

Week 1	Body Analogy-Scripture-body's value, price paid; Circulation-terminology-function, heart, blood components-cells , shape-function; Respiration
Week 2	Injuries and Healing-Components of Blood-plasma, nutrients and minerals, leukocytes, granulocytes, thrombocytes, platelets, fibrinogen, antigen, lymphocytes, antibodies; Immunity-response to infection, creating antibodies, lymph system , science catches up with the Bible
Week 3	Skeletal System-composition and function of the skeleton; Muscles– function-types; Joints, ligaments, tendons; The Hand
Week 4	Digestive System– Organs, Fluids and Functions
Week 5	Nervous System– Brain
Week 6	Reproductive System DNA/ Life's Origins
Week 7	Five Senses-auditory, vision, olfactory and taste, tactile and skin; Language
Week 8	Races; Human History Round-up— Oral presentations of students "big" project Celebrate God's gift of the body.

Lesson Plans

Subject Date:	Monday	Tuesday	Wednesday	Thursday	Friday
Bible/Religion Studies					
Teaching Outline					
Reading Section					
Language Arts/Spelling/ Vocabulary					
Math Reinforcement					
Science Activities and Experiments					
Geography/History					
Art/Music					

CR= Creation Resource   TS= Teacher Selection

Lesson Plan Grades 9-12 Week 1

Bible/ Religion Studies—Monday-Wednesday: Cor. 12:12-27 (dictation / memory work) **Thursday– Friday** Lev 17 Gen 2: 7 and verses of your choice dealing with blood/ heart and breathe. Show how to use a Concordance to find other related verses.

Morning warm up: 5 minute write up! (optional) Do this everyday and you will be surprise how quickly you kids will love it and their writing will improve! This is a great way to get past writer's block. Anything they write in 5 minutes is shared at the end. Here's how it works: Give your student a topic or word you choose and 5 minutes to write —what ever comes into their head. Here's a few topics that are popping into my head, for example: how or if a foot can get along without the rest of the body or how is your body unique, or what is your favorite body part and why or what do you want to learn about the body, or how do you think food effects the body, or how can you make a body stronger or grow taller or faster or can you? Words like: heartache, the blood of Christ, pumping, and breath. This is just a quick exercise and the children will get better and better at it each day. They don't ponder the topic they just pick up their pen/pencil and write. My kids balked at first, but by the end of the first week, they were begging for more time to finish! They wrote short stories, poems, songs and many silly sentences! It doesn't matter the point is to get the creative juices flowing and to get it on paper! (Additional 5 minute write-up ideas: love, sacrifice, obedience, medicine, feet, exercise, doctor, emergency, experiment, determination)

Teaching Outline– Monday: I a,b,c, II-a,b,c,d **Tuesday** –Review II-d, continued **Wednesday**- II-e **Thursday**-Review II a-e **Friday** –Review knowledge

Reading / Research- Every day: For upper grades reading and research is the primary way students make their learning their own. Teachers are more the facilitator, guide and enabler. Work with student closely to select the exceptional books that will go deeper into this unit. For more hands-on learners, model building, experiments and diagram drawing will be beneficial.

Language Arts Spelling Vocabulary and Grammar-

Monday- As you read the Teaching Outline and your resource books select the vocabulary words pertaining to this week's study. Assign unknown words to look up and write definitions. Look at the origins of the vocabulary words (Spelling/ Vocabulary and Grammar Ideas 9-12). Have the student make an oral presentation about the human body as related to the Body of Christ (Language Arts Ideas 9-12).

Tuesday-To make sure the older students have knowledge of easier vocabulary ask them to make word puzzles for the younger students (Spelling/Vocabulary Pull sentences from the books they are reading for dictation, sentence structure and sentence diagramming.

Wednesday– Have student write a biographical sketch of a scientist of interest in this study. Check spelling and sentence structure/grammar.

Thursday-Review vocabulary to make sure they have learned the definitions; Write a comparison between body, soul and spirit (Language Arts 9-12)

Friday-Review vocabulary, spelling.

Math Reinforcement/ Science Activities and Experiments/ Geography/ History / Art/ Music/ Drama- Using your resources both in this guide and those you have found in the library, bookstores, and internet put together your students integrated curriculum plan of attack.

How are you going to approach this study with the older student? Depending on the depth and length of the study you are planning you can approach this for students in the upper grades differently. You might choose a more in depth study or a more generalized approach depending on the interest level of the student. A more in depth study could result in a larger, more sophisticated (science fair quality) project on a specific area of interest. If you choose this route, be sure to include daily oral updates on what they are reading (should be several types of sources) and reviewing the notes they are taking. This project should includes experiments using the scientific method, and possibly interviews with people. Demand excellence in the finish writing product, with rewrites as necessary. Choosing the in depth study should also have the benefit of attaining a general knowledge of the interactive workings of the entire body. If you select a more generalize study of anatomy, it should demonstrate some depth of knowledge as to how our bodies work. It might include a more historical approach by studying the history of medicine, the scientists who toiled to advance our knowledge of the body, and the part medicine has played in improving the lives of people, and societies. A study of medical ethics is a possibility.

**Remember: Read it; watch it (or follow the processes by a diagram); review it; have the student tell it back to you orally and in writing, drawing or modeling projects and experiments. Choose different types of writing too, like poetry, dramatic portrayals, consider options like an informational speech, public service announcements that are video taped or power point demonstrations.

Monday: Using the Teaching Outline Read/Teach from the outline about the value both spiritually and materially of the Human Body. Watch the Red River of Life DVD as an introduction to the circulatory system . Discuss the movie in light of 1 Cor. 12-12-27 and being members of the body of Christ. What is the value of the human body in relation to its elements? (Math Reinforcement Ideas 9-12). Write out the chemical name for Hemoglobin, and explain each of the chemical symbols (Science Activities and Experiments 9-12). What is the difference between an atom, an element and a molecule (Science Activities and Experiments 9-12). Describe the unique transportation system of the blood. Begin charting your pulse at different times of the day (Math Reinforcement Ideas 9-12) Start an exercise program and see how it effects your heart rate over the course of the unit (Science Activities and Experiments 9-12). Spend extra time reading the books you have selected to read individually for the study. How will you share what you have learned about the blood, heart, arteries and veins? (Report, term paper, informational speech, power point, can you add demonstrations/ experiments?);

Tuesday-Read and teach from the outline. Can you explain how the blood travels through the heart and is circulated through the body. What is the function and structure of the system. Review the parts of the heart and blood vessels. Demonstrate osmosis (Science Activities and Experiments 4-8). Continue to spend extra time reading and taking notes for your project. Look into the life and times of scientists who contributed to our understanding of the heart and blood. Learn and explain how understanding has changed and look at what was happening historically at the time to see if that influenced their research. Try to get different animal hearts from the butcher to compare, cut in half and identify the chambers.

Wednesday– Review from the teaching outline vocabulary, and the circulation process. Can the students tell the process to you? Continue your study of the blood and its make up and respiration. How many breaths do you take in one day? (Math Reinforcement Ideas 4-8) What comprises the air we breathe (Math Reinforcement Ideas 4-8). Review the process oxygen goes through after it is inhaled and passes through the cells, organs, and is carried to the lungs and exhaled (Science Activities and Experiments 4-8). On a white board or chalk board map out the process of respiration and how the fuel (oxygen) travels through the body and how the waste is removed and expelled through the lungs. Explain diffusion (Blood and Guts). How are the lungs of scuba divers effected during dives. What happens when divers come too quickly to the surface? What are the effects of smoking on the lungs? Write and perform a public service announcement that would or might help convince people to quick smoking. Use the Teaching Outline to make Trivia Cards (Science Activities and Experiments 4-8). Make up a game using the cards. What has your historical research on the scientists uncovered? Who was Walter Reed and what contributions did he make?

Thursday-: Continue to add cards to the Trivia Game you have created to review the material. Continue your research and reading. Work on your projects-both written and hands-on. What are the parts of the Circulatory System you find most interesting? What are questions you still have? Where can you look to find the answers? Have you been taking a historical perspective studying the life and times of the scientists who shaped the knowledge we have of the Circulatory and Respiratory Systems? Tell what you have learned.

Friday: Review all material covered this week. How best can your student recap what learning has taken place? Have the students make presentation of materials, experiments, models, and drawings so they can demonstrate their knowledge. Consider inviting friends in to listen to the presentations. Have there been any changes on their pulse rates and exercise charts since they began at the beginning of the week? Continue this charting for the entire unit. Play your Trivia Game. Thank God always for the gift of our bodies and pray that we always be mindful that our bodies are a temple of the Holy Spirit.

Lesson Plan Grades 9-12 Week 2

Bible/ Religion Studies—Teacher's choice of verses and lessons

Morning warm up: 5 minute write up! A few quick ideas— but let YOUR imagination go and think of some of your own starters: scar, sneeze, skinned knees, red, stitches, germs, shots

Teaching Outline-Monday-Review, III-a1-3 **Tuesday-**III-a1-7 **Wednesday-**III-b1-4 **Thursday**– Review, **Friday**– reports and presentations

Reading/Research—Every day: Depending on the depth of the projects this could be 2-3 hours per day.

Language Arts, Spelling, Vocabulary and Grammar—

Monday: assign vocabulary and writing definitions on index cards, write sentences for them; Research a scientist like Louis Pasteur and write biological sketch (Language Arts 9-12)

Tuesday: review words, definitions , continue to work on biological sketch.

Wednesday: review words, dictate paragraph that contains vocabulary words (Language Arts 9-12). Look up origins of vocabulary (Spelling/Vocabulary and grammar Ideas 9-12). Why was Latin a good language for scientific nomenclature? (Language Arts 9-12).

Thursday: review definitions of vocabulary, rewrite the biological sketch to make it prefect.

Friday: Read your biological sketch

Math Reinforcement/ Science Activities and Experiments/ Geography/ History / Art/ Music/ Drama-

Monday: Review material from last week especially pertaining to blood cells. Add more Trivia Cards; Continue with the exercise program started last week: keep a record of your heart rate; Continue to read books on our unit and assign appropriate ways to report what they are learning; If it is a biography, for history/ geography integration check a map or globe for where the scientist lived and what was happening in history at the time of his work. What is Plasma? Do some research to get a good definition of this life saving fluid. How do antibodies and proteins in plasma fight infections? What is Plasmapheresis? Begin deeper research on a topic of interest concerning blood: hemophilia, leukemia, etc.

Tuesday: Study a cut or scrape of someone in your home and monitor of the healing process (Science Activities and Experiments K-3) Where are the blood cells made? What are the functions of each. Draw these cells and tell how they differ. What does Bible say about diseases and cleanliness? Prepare cleanliness survey (Math Reinforcement Ideas 4-8.)

Wednesday: What is the difference between bacteria and virus. Grow bacteria. Use caution here when growing bacteria! Who discovered penicillin? What can you discover about him and how he made this discovery. Research Louis Pasteur and his "germ theory." Where did he come from? What is spontaneous generation? (Science Activities and Experiments 9-12) Recreate Louis Pasteur's experiment with chicken broth. Who are the other scientists who contributed to the creation of antibiotics and vaccines. Research Borelli burgdorferi (lymes disease); Write copy for a commercial or public service announcement about the importance of getting a flu shot, about some other health issue. Think of sound effects to put with the copy. What is the recovery time from various illnesses? (Math Reinforcement Ideas 9-12) What are antigens and antibodies? Learn about immunizations. Why are some people today refusing to vaccinate? Is this irresponsible in your opinion? What could be the consequences to society? Write a paper that would argue for or against.

Thursday: Continue to work on your PSA. Can you film it? Continue to work on other research, papers, speeches, presentations that demonstrate what you have learned in this unit. Check your experiments and write your observations.

Friday: How best can you some up what you have learned about the healing process this week? If you did a major experiment or wrote a paper make a presentation. If you made a commercial, perform it or video tape it and share it with friends. Tell about a scientist you have studied this week and their contribution.

Lesson Plan Grades 9-12 Week 3

Bible/ Religion Studies— Job 10: 8-11; Teacher's choice of verses and lessons

Morning warm up: 5 minute write up! A few quick ideas— but let YOUR imagination go and think of some of your own starters: bones, movement, muscles, joints, ghost limbs, physical therapy

Teaching Outline-Monday-IV-a, b **Tuesday-**IV-c1,2 **Wednesday-**IV-d, e **Thursday–** Review Continue with projects/experiments **Friday–** reports and presentations

Reading/Research—Every day: Depending on the depth of the projects this could be 2-3 hours per day.

Language Arts, Spelling, Vocabulary and Grammar—

Monday assign vocabulary and writing definitions on index cards, write sentences for them; Learn the spelling.

Tuesday review words, definitions. Find someone in the field of physical therapy to interview and write a newspaper article based on it.

Wednesday review words and definitions. Review your newspaper article and look at ways to improve it grammatically, or turn it into a speech or even a power point presentation.

Thursday review definitions of vocabulary. Continue to work on your project.

Friday– Check knowledge of vocabulary spelling and definitions.

Math Reinforcement/ Science Activities and Experiments/ Geography/ History / Art/ Music/ Drama-

Monday– Read through the teaching outline on the Skeletal and Muscular Systems and the other resource books you have. Choose the experiments and activities. Add more Trivia Cards; Continue with the exercise program started the first week: keep record of your heart rate; Are you picking one area this week to really dig deeply into with research and experiments? Are you studying a particular scientist who contributed to our knowledge of the human body? Bones get some strength from their cylindrical shape (Science Activities and Experiments for grades 9-12). Why are the bones like this? How do you keep your bones strong? (Science Activities and Experiments for K-3) What happens when minerals are removed from bones. Look at the crystalline structure of calcium and phosphorous atoms as it relates to bone strength (Science Activities and Experiments 9-12). Memorize the names of the major bones in the body. Make a diagram of a cross section of a bone. Look at a real bone to compare—use a soup bone. Bones need calcium and vitamin D. Why are women more prone to osteoporosis? How about men? What is necessary for building strong bones? Do you get enough calcium? How about Mom? Look for people who may have osteoporosis, describe the effects. A particularly interesting area is the work being done in prosthetics (artificial limbs). What is a phantom limb? Continue to read books on our unit and assign appropriate ways to report about what they are learning; If it is a biography, for history/geography integration check a map or globe for where the scientist lived and what was happening in history at the time of his work.

Tuesday– Identify and classify muscles (Science Activities and Experiments 9-12). What does the word mouse have to do with muscle? Make a drawing or find a picture of the different types of muscles. How do the muscles differ from each other. Build a model of the arm (Science Activities and Experiments 4-8) or in Linda Allison's Blood and Guts. Explain how the muscles make the arm move (extend and contract). Learn which pairs of muscles work in opposition to each other (Science Activities and Experiments 9-12). Find the connective fibers by examining a piece of steak.

Wednesday-Kinesiology is the study of body movement. Research what this is about. How does it relate to dance or physical therapy? Do dissection of a chicken thigh (Science Activities and Experiments 4-8). Look at the joint of chicken wing or thigh and leg joints. Identify and classify the types of joints. Use a large can of vegetables and place it in one hand. Squeeze and release the can and feel the tendons in your arm (Science Activities and Experiments 4-8).

Thursday-Continue to work on your projects, and bring them to conclusion determining how best to demonstrate the knowledge learned. Where do you need more work—writing or oral presentations or power point preparation? Look at a first aid book and learn some basics of first aid, especially as it pertains to broken bone, and sprains.

Friday– Complete your research experiments and projects. Present your papers, research and experiments and demonstrate your knowledge! Play your Trivia Game.

Lesson Plans 9-12 Week 4

Bible/ Religion Studies— Genesis 1:29-30 Teacher's choice of verses and lessons

Morning warm up: 5 minute write up! A few quick ideas— but let YOUR imagination go and think of some of your own starters: stomach, enzymes, swallow, chew, favorite food, choke

Teaching Outline-Monday-V-a, b, c **Tuesday-**V-a, b, c **Wednesday-**V-a, b, c **Thursday**– Review **Friday**– reports and presentations

Reading—Every day: Depending on the depth of the projects this could be 2-3 hours per day.

Language Arts, Spelling, Vocabulary—

Monday assign vocabulary and writing definition on index cards. Look up the words in a dictionary, science dictionary or encyclopedia and write the words and a brief definition of each. Then have him write the words in complete sentences using as many parts of speech as he can. Have him use a thesaurus. Learn the spelling. Research the topic of obesity in America or anorexia.

Tuesday review words, definitions, continue to work on your research and perhaps find someone in the field to interview.

Wednesday review words, turn your research into a paper of some form or a speech or even a power point presentation.

Thursday review definitions of vocabulary, continue to work on your "project" to make it prefect.

Friday– make a presentation of your project.

Math Reinforcement/Science Activities and Experiments/Geography/History/Art/Music/Drama-

Monday-Read through the section on Digestive System and The Body Book as you make your plan of study and what area students want to dig deeper so that they start their research today! For example the liver is a most amazing organ because it can repair itself if damaged! From your books read about the mouth, tongue, saliva, teeth and what happens when you bite into an apple or bagel. Discuss the concept of food as fuel and why eating good food is important, especially fruits and vegetables. (Gen. 1:29-30) Chew a salty cracker well without swallowing it (Science Activities and Experiments K–3). Diagram the inside of the mouth. Note where the saliva glands are. What enzymes are released?

Do some research on hunger in the world, marking a map of particular areas where people are suffering and what is being done to help them (Geography/ History Ideas 4-8).

Tuesday– The esophagus, stomach and liver are the topics. Check your resource books for information, models to build and experiments, like Janice Van Cleave's The Human Body for Everykid, or The Body Book: Easy Models that Teach, by Donald Silver and Patricia J. Wynne and The Human Body: 25 Fantastic Project, by Kathleen Reilly. Measure the amount of food you eat in a day. (See Math Reinforcement Ideas 4-8) What foods give you the most energy? (See Science Activities and Experiments: 4 -8) Plan a menu and analyze the nutritional information (Science Activities and Experiments 9-12). Research the uniqueness of the liver or the way the ideas of healthy eating has changed since the Middle Ages and prepare a presentation for Friday (Geography/History ideas 9-12).

Wednesday–How long does it take for food to travel through the digestive system? (Math Reinforcement Ideas 9-12) If you lay out the intestines how long are they? What are the percentages of water loss? (Math Reinforcement Ideas 9-12) Continue to work on the experiments and models you have selected and be sure to prepare in writing or for oral presentation the learning that has taken place.

Thursday– Finish working on projects and reports for presentations on Friday.

Friday– Make presentations and reports, show models and experiments data and result as per the Scientific Method Sheets.

Lesson Plans 9-12 Week 5

Bible/ Religion Studies— Phil. 4:8, Study the book of Romans as it applies to thinking rightly Roman 12:2 Teacher's choice of verses and lessons

Morning warm up: 5 minute write up! A few quick ideas— but let YOUR imagination go and think of some of your own starters: brain, smart, intelligence, imagine, dream, understanding, balance.

Teaching Outline-Monday-Parts of the Brain, Cerebrum (largest part), cerebellum (balance) **Tuesday**– Pituitary gland, brainstem (involuntary activities), hypothalamus, thalamus **Wednesday**– Spinal Cord and Nerves **Thursday**– Review **Friday**– reports and presentations

Reading—Every day: Depending on the depth of the projects this could be 2-3 hours per day.

Language Arts, Spelling, Vocabulary—

Monday assign vocabulary and writing definition on index cards. Look up the words in a dictionary, science dictionary or encyclopedia and write the words and a brief definition of each. Write the words in complete sentences using as many parts of speech as possible. Have him use a thesaurus. Learn the spelling. Do research about what's being done on ADHD, Cerebral Palsy, or Alzheimer's Disease.

Tuesday review words, definitions, continue to work on your research and perhaps find someone in the field to interview.

Wednesday review words, turn your research into a paper of some form or a speech or a power point presentation.

Thursday review definitions of vocabulary, continue to work on your "project" to make it prefect.

Friday– make a presentation of your project.

Math Reinforcement/Science Activities and Experiments/Geography/History/ Art/Music/Drama-

Monday-Read through the Teaching Outline section on the brain and nervous system and The Body Book by Steve Parker as you make your plan of study. Some suggestions for deeper investigation might be: effects of stroke, work of a physical /occupational therapist or neuropsychologist, understanding how pathways are formed when learning new tasks, epilepsy, cerebral palsy, Alzheimer disease, growth problems in children, or spinal cord injuries. Diagram the brain parts and learn the function of the cerebrum and cerebellum. What is left brain right brain dominance? Choose one of the art projects, like using different color clay to make a model of the brain (Art/Music 4-8).

Tuesday– Locate the thalamus, hypothalamus, pituitary gland and the brain stem. Learn about what activities they control. Chart the different areas of your brain that control your actions (Science Activities and Experiments: 9-12). What causes you to grow, and mature? Hormones! Do some research on hormones and their importance to our health. The Pituitary gland controlled by the hypothalamus release the hormones that allow this to happen. The brain stem is the control center for involuntary actions (like breathing, heart beat, and other organ functions). Discuss and read your resource books concerning these parts of the brain. Play some memory games. Continue to work on reports or research projects. Do some research about the use of growth hormones in sports and how sports has changed because of it. Look at the legality as well as the moral aspects. What danger does it pose to youth to see pro athletes abusing their bodies. Is there an argument for "Choice" here?

Wednesday–The spinal cord and nerves are the body's messaging system. Study the Braille system. How does this relate to the nervous system? (Science Activities and Experiments: 9-12) What are nerves and neurons? How do nerves help in the learning of new tasks. Check your students reaction time (Science Activities and Experiments K-3). Many brain and spinal cord injuries occur during car accidents and during sports or recreational activities. How can we protect our brain? Continue to spend time researching your topic.

Thursday– Test your student's memory by giving another blank diagram of the brain and see if your students can name all the parts. Test short term memory and find out about long term memory and the effects of alcohol and drugs. Choose further experiments from your resource book like Janice Van Cleave's Human Body for Every Kid and Janice Van Cleave's Biology for Every Kid, and The Human Body: 25 Fantastic Projects. Continue to compile your research on your topic of special interest. Plan how you can best share your information.

Friday– Wrap up the week with reports, oral presentations, summaries of experiments, and memory games.

Lesson Plans Grades 9-12 Week 6

Bible/ Religion Studies— Monday-Friday-Gen. 1: 26, Gen. 1:28, Ps. 139:14
Teacher's choice of verses and lessons

Morning warm up: 5 minute write up! A few quick ideas— but let YOUR imagination go and think of some of your own starters: truth, falsehood, embryo, baby, evolution, creation, designer baby, cloning, abortion.

Teaching Outline-Monday-Evolution /Creation debate **Tuesday**– Human Reproduction **Wednesday**– Genetics, **Thursday**– DNA **Friday**– reports and presentations

Reading—Every day: Depending on the depth of the projects this could be 2-3 hours per day.

Language Arts, Spelling, Vocabulary—

Monday assign words and writing definitions on index cards. Look up the words in a dictionary, science dictionary or encyclopedia and write the words and a brief definition of each. Write the words in complete sentences using as many parts of speech as possible. Create a headline and lead newspaper story with the findings that the Creations Story is true (Language Arts 9-12). Learn the spelling.

Tuesday review words, definitions. Study the origins of words; Research how the use of words by people in power were used to dehumanize other groups of people and what the results were.

Wednesday review words, turn your research into a paper of some form or a speech or even a power point presentation.

Thursday review definitions of vocabulary, continue to work on your "project" to make it prefect.

Friday– make a presentation of your project. Stage a Creation/Evolution debate (Language Arts 9-12).

Math Reinforcement/Science Activities and Experiments/Geography/History/ Art/Music/Drama

Monday-Read through the section on the Reproduction and DNA from the Teaching Outline paying close attention to the flaws of evolution theory. We have chosen to begin our study at the stage of union of egg and sperm and the beginning of a new single-cell person. It is the parent's prerogative as to what additional information and how to present this information to the student. After reading the outline, what topics piques your student's interest? What are some ways of researching this, and how are you going to share this information? How about the student teaching it as a lesson?

The outline begins with flaws of evolutionary thinking that demonstrate that the evolution being taught as fact is really only a theory not proven science and it has serious defects. Take time if you have not studied this debate before to cover it. Give your students the tools and understanding to point out the flaws of evolution when they are challenged by friends from the public school. Check out resources from our reading list and those found at: www.tccsa.tc/books (Twin Cities Creation Science Association) for an awesome book list. Science in Creation Week by David Unfred has some hands on experiments. The fossil record contradicts the theory of evolution. How so? (Science Activities and Experiment 9-12) .

Tuesday– Life begins at fertilization. Familiarize yourself with the development of the fetus (which means little one) by tracing it's development from fertilization through the first year after birth. Make some drawings of the path a fertilized egg takes and it's development. Refer to your reference books like Steve Parker's The Human Body Book reading the sections on human embryonic development. If you haven't introduced your young person to the pro-life movement now is a great time. One of the repercussions of evolutionary thought is the loss of dignity and respect for the human being. If human life came about by chance and there is no purpose for our existence, then terminating a pregnancy becomes an easier choice. However, if every life is an eternal gift from God, who are we to reject that gift and kill our small brother or sister terminating that life becomes unthinkable? For Pro-Life Resources go to Priests for Life, Human Life International, Rock for Life, and The Center for Bioethical Reform. The pro-life movement is the greatest moral and civil rights movement of our time! Consider researching and reporting information about some aspect of the pro-life effort. Research the Genocide Awareness Project (this will be shocking for the sensitive student so Parental preview is strongly suggested).

Wednesday– Read about genes and heredity. Look up the Scientist, Fr. Gregor Johann Mendel, and the work on genetics. Can you predict the combination of traits of offspring of two parents by make at chart like Mendel's? What is DNA? What does it stand for and how is it related to the work of Mendel. Write a short report on this scientist's contributions. Mendel was an "Austrian monk," but actually he was born in what is now called the Czech Republic. Look at the map and write a "side bar" article about the map of Europe in 1822 and the Austro-Hungarian Empire. How did Isaac Newton invent calculus? (Math Reinforcement

Ideas 9-12) Study the work of Sir Francis Crick and how that work changed his mind about evolution. (Science Activities and Experiments 9-12)

Thursday-Continue the research started yesterday on DNA, chromosomes, and genes. What is the Genome Project? Construct a Lego DNA molecule. (Science Activities and Experiments:4-8) Read through the section on DNA and research something that captures your curiosity. Takes notes and plan an oral presentation for Friday.

Friday– Review the weeks findings and make presentations, go over research and discuss/debate the creation/evolution theories. Share your research in some way.

Lesson Plans Grades 9-12 Week 7

Bible/ Religion Studies— Monday-Friday Psalms 33:18, Psalms 119:103, Proverbs 1:8, Phil 4:18, Mark 5:28, Gen 11:19 or Teacher's choice.

Morning warm up: 5 minute write up! A few quick ideas— but let YOUR imagination go and think of some of your own starters: blindness (physical or spiritual), deafness, sign language, sensitivity, babble.

Teaching Outline-Monday-5 senses **Tuesday**– 5 senses **Wednesday**– Language **Thursday**– Language **Friday**– reports and presentations

Reading—Every day: Depending on the depth of the projects this could be 2-3 hours per day.

Language Arts, Spelling, Vocabulary

Monday assign words and writing definitions on index cards. , Look up the words in a dictionary, science dictionary or encyclopedia and write the words and a brief definition of each. Write the words in complete sentences using as many parts of speech as possible. Learn the spelling.

Tuesday use the words in a sentence. Do the activity describing a sunset if you were color blind. (Language Arts Ideas 4-8)

Wednesday write the harder words several in row with only one spelled correctly and see if student can pick out the correct spelling. Select a paragraph for dictation and sentence for diagraming.

Thursday-spell words orally.

Friday– Review, take the spelling test.

Math Reinforcement/Science Activities and Experiments/Geography/History/Art/Music/Drama

Monday-Read through the section on the Senses. Let students choose one or two senses to become "experts" on and begin doing research. Decide how this research will be presented on Friday. Consider doing research on sign language or learning braille especially if you have studied the senses in the past and they know the parts of and functions already. Look deeper into the uniqueness of human language and how complex our communications really are compared to animals ability to communicate. Decide now what mode of reporting your learning will take on Friday. Using your resources have the students read about eyes and sight, ears and hearing and mouth and taste. Check your resource books for experiments and possible activities for these senses.

Tuesday—Using resources read about the nose and smelling, and skin and touch. Check these books for experiments and possible activities for these senses. Try the experiment about the relationship between taste and smell (Science Activities and Experiments 9-12). Don't forget to make diagrams and label them. Do the experiment about melanin. (Science Activities and Experiments 4-8). Observe dead skin cells with a magnifying glass (Science Activities and Experiments 4-8). Do the experiment to see if you are waterproof (Science Activities and Experiments:4 -8). Study the art of fingerprinting (Geography and History Ideas 4-8). Make thumbprint art (Art/Music K-3). Measure the surface area of the skin of your body. Devise different ways to do this (Math reinforcement Ideas 4–8). How were the bodies of ancient Egyptian mummies prepared for burial? Why did this treatment preserve the skin? (Geography and History Ideas 4-8).

Wednesday– Read from the Teaching Outline about Language, don't forget to read the account in the Bible, Gen. 11: 19. Research the origin of languages (Geography/History Ideas 4-8). Using a blank world map, chart the locations of the different languages (Geography/History4-8) Learn some basic phrases in another language. Recall what part of the brain contains the language functions. Research how victims of strokes go about relearning speech.

Thursday– Make a chart of different consonant sound. (Science Activities and Experiments; 4-8). Prepare your presentation of what you have learned this week. Make Trivia cards for your Trivia Game so that you can play it on Friday with your family.

Friday– Give oral reports, demonstration of experiments, projects that were done this week. Play your Trivia Game.

Lesson Plans Grades 9-12 Week 8

Bible/ Religion Studies— Teacher's choice.

Morning warm up: 5 minute write up! A few quick ideas— but let YOUR imagination go and think of some of your own starters: pigment, dignity, racism, fairness, population, inventions, prejudice, technology, intelligence.

Teaching Outline-Monday-Race **Tuesday**– Human History **Wednesday**– Technology **Thursday**– Review and preparation of papers/ projects **Friday**– reports and presentations.

Reading—Every day: Depending on the depth of the projects this could be 2-3 hours per day.

Language Arts, Spelling, Vocabulary

Monday assign words and writing definitions on index cards. Look up the words in a dictionary, science dictionary or encyclopedia and write the words and a brief definition of each. Write the words in complete sentences using as many parts of speech as he can. Learn the spelling.

Tuesday Study the origins of the vocabulary words (Spelling/Vocabulary and Grammar Ideas 9-12). Use the vocabulary words for a word search puzzle.

Wednesday write the harder words several in row with only one spelled correctly and see if student can pick out the correct spelling. Select a paragraph for dictation and sentence for diagraming.

Thursday-spell words orally.

Friday– Review. Take the spelling test.

Math Reinforcement/Science Activities and Experiments/Geography/History/ Art/Music/Drama

Monday-Read through the section on the Races. Do the bandage on the finger exercise (Science Activities and Experiments 4-8). What skin types have a higher concentration of melanin? Check out your resources, like Of Pandas and People and research the influence evolution has had on the equality of the races. Do some research on racial prejudices and write a paper on the damage this type of thinking has caused in society and in our world. Look at how the Nazi portrayed the Jews to see how words and pictures (cartoons) can influence people's perceptions of

158

others. Check out the connection between racism and the founder of Planned Parenthood. Look into the way propaganda and especially the way words can be used to dehumanize a group of people. If you haven't already done so, look at the Genocide Awareness Project and research how and why they are using visuals to attempt to turn public opinion toward the sanctity of life. How effective do you think this is? What form of reporting are you going to use in reporting your learning? Posters and visuals might be useful.

Tuesday-Read the section on Human History about population. Research the population explosion claims and on the claims of those who say the earth is not over-populated (Geography/History 9-12). What are your opinions? What is a one world government? (Geography/History 9-12).

Wednesday– Today look at the inventions throughout human history. Choose an invention to research (Geography/History 4-8) Study the history of anatomy (Geography/History 9-12). Create at time line of the great discoveries of medicine. Sometimes people today think they are more intelligent than those who lived earlier in history. Do you believe this? Research the learning requirements at different times in History for students your age. How is it different or the same as what you are required to know.

Thursday-Choose one of the areas you have been researching this week to put more effort into today and add more information and decide how you will present your learning on Friday. Choose a method that will showcase your topic.

Friday- Make a summary report of this week's learning and make your final report/ presentation. Take a look back over the information, exercises, experiments, and activities you have been doing these last 8 weeks and marvel at all you have accomplished and learned. What is one area or topic that you have learned the most? Celebrate the gift of life.

Reading List
9-12

*Books may be difficult to find in the library but are available on Amazon or eBay for very good prices.

Adam and Evolution by Michael Pitman
        Publisher: Rider and Co, 1984, 268 pp. (new and used copies   through Amazon.com)
        This book is written by a biology professor who is not a fundamentalist Christian. He has nevertheless come to the conclusion that there has never been any evolution and that man was specially created. Very interesting reading!

Designs in the Living World by Lane Lester
        Publisher: SimBioSys, 1997, pp. 254. (Used copies on Amazon.com)
        Have you ever wished for an excellent high school level Biology textbook in which the author's view reflects young-earth creation? Well here it is! This gem contains factual material in text-book format. It has chapters dealing with genetics, cell division, development of life, origins of life and much more. As if that were not enough, it also includes a Biology lab manual!

Isaac Newton: Mastermind of Modern Science by David C. Knight.
        Publisher: Franklin Watts, 1961, 153 pp. (Used copies on Amazon.com)
        Isaac Newton contributed much to science, not only in the discovery   of gravity. This book is about his life and his contributions.

Speculations and Experiments on the Origin of Life by Duane Gish
        Publisher: New Leaf Pr, 1972 (out of print– used copies on Amazon.com)
        A somewhat technical book dealing with the questions of the origin   of life. Some experiments and activities help to form a better understanding.

Soldier Doctor by Clara Judson (used copies available through Amazon.com)
        Publisher: Scribner, 1942. Complete review on 4-8 reading list.

Activity and Experiment
Resource List
9-12

Bill Nye The Science Guy's Big Blast of Science by Bill Nye
    Publisher: Basic Books, 1993, 176 pp.
    A book which discusses the fundamentals of science in a format that appeals to teens. Uses the scientific method and contains many experiments. This book covers many of the ancient scientists, their discoveries, and experiments to re-create them.

How the Body Works by Steve Parker
    Publisher: Dorling Kindersley Publishers Ltd, 1999, 192 pp.
    (See complete review on page 59) While there are many activities that require building or complicated projects, this should be a book high school students can do on their own.

Of Pandas and People: The Central Question of Biological Origins by
    Percival Davis, Dean H. Kenyon and Charles B. Thaxton
    Publisher: Haughton Publishing Company, 1989, 1993, 166 pp.
    This book took quite a while to publish. It was given to many people to read, comment on, suggest ideas for, and question. It is not light reading. If there was a recommended Biology textbook for the Creation Science classroom, this would be it. It is written on two levels; one is for an overview of the topic; the other is a more in-depth look. This was done to present the material to students of various ages.

The Body Book (Book & DVD), by Steve Parker, DK: New York Editor Jill
    Hamilton, 2007.

The Human Body: 25 Fantastic Project, by Kathleen Reilly, White River
    Junction, VT: Nomad Press, 2008.

Usborne Illustrated Dictionary of Science by Corinne Stockley, Chris Oxlade, and Jane Wertheim
    Publisher: Usborne Books, 2007, 382 pp.
    Although this book claims to be a dictionary, it is has the clearest definitions of physics, chemistry and biology facts I have seen. It contains the periodic table, and drawings of DNA molecules, cells and much more. It is a colorful text that really explains complicated subjects well.

Internet sites:

History World: http://www.hyperhistory.com/

Creation Anatomy: Video and additional information:

Creation Website: http://www.icr.org/creation-anatomy

Vocabulary/Spelling List

9-12

These words are used as a base for your vocabulary and spelling list. If the vocabulary words are unknown, have the child research them either in a dictionary, science dictionary, or as a last resort, but I know you will use it — online!

adaptation	deoxyribonucleic acid	medulla	porphyrin
alveoli	dominant trait	meninges	phagocytosis
amylase	duodenum	pia mater	pons
antibodies	erythrocytes	arachnoid	receptors
antigens	extensors	dura mater	ribonucleic acid
appendicular skeleton	expiration	metabolism	ribosomes
axial skeleton	fibrin	myocardium	septum
biogenesis	fibrinogen	nucleotides	stasis
biomechanics	flexors	occipital lobe	stereo cilia
bronchioles	frontal lobe	olfactory	temporal lobe
cardiac	ganglion	osteoblasts	thalamus
cecum	hemoglobin	parietal lobe	thrombocytes
cerebellum	homology	pericardium	trait
chromosomes	hypothalamus	perilymph fluid	dominant
coronary	immunities	periosteum	recessive
cytoplasm	inspiration	pleurae	tricuspid valve
			villi (villus)

Spelling/Vocabulary and Grammar Ideas
9-12

◊ Use the vocabulary and spelling words interchangeably in the following activities.

◊ A pre-test of spelling and vocabulary is a good indication of the words your child already knows. Dictate the words orally, or by audio cassette, and let him spell the words and write a brief definition.

◊ Have your child look up the words that he does not know in a dictionary, science dictionary or encyclopedia and write the words and a brief definition of each. Then have him write the words in complete sentences using as many parts of speech as he can. Have him use a thesaurus.

◊ Use the sentences to label and diagram the parts of speech. Refer to a language book, if necessary.

◊ Test to see that he knows the definitions of the vocabulary words. Use different formats: oral test, multiple choice, true or false, etc.

◊ Study the origins of the vocabulary words. What is the language of their origins? Were their original meanings the same as their meanings today? (You may not be able to find this information in a standard dictionary.)

◊ Have your child make up original crossword puzzles. Try to use words that are difficult to remember. Use around ten to twelve words for each puzzle. He can give these to adults to work out, then check the answers! Have older children make puzzles for younger children using age appropriate vocabulary words.

◊ Use the vocabulary words for a word search puzzle. Make it more difficult by putting words in backwards and diagonally.

◊ Make a "body" game. Use construction paper and make spaces around the perimeter (or any way you wish). Put in obstacles like "flu: lose a turn", etc. Place the vocabulary words on the spaces and number them. Give each word (depending on its difficulty) a number of spaces you can move. For example, if you land on the space containing the word "immunities" and correctly define the word, you can move two spaces. If the word was "osteoblasts" and it was correctly defined, you might move five spaces. Make up vocabulary answer sheets corresponding to the numbered vocabulary words on the board for an easy reference. This is a great way to learn difficult words.

◊ Make a word calendar, complete with definitions and illustrations. Learn one new word a day. This is a great vocabulary builder.

Language Arts Ideas
9-12

◊ Use 1 Cor. 12:12-27 as a basis for an oral presentation of the human body and the way it works and its relation to believers as the Body of Christ.

◊ Research different scientists. Pick a scientist of interest. Write a biographical sketch of this person's life. What type of education was necessary for his degree? How many years of school, etc.? What was sacrificed (family, time, religion) in the quest for knowledge? Were the sacrifices worth it in your estimation? In God's? (Do the same activity as an autobiography. Another variation is to add fictionalized accounts or write as if you lived in the future.)

◊ Use a first aid book and learn the basics of first aid. Write a small pamphlet and illustrate it showing different treatments you can use in case of emergency.

◊ Research hypothermia. What are ways to prevent it in case of emergency? Focus on survival skills for cold climates, and on water temperatures. Should you ever stay in one place until help comes?

◊ Using a paragraph from a book you are reading for dictation, check for proper spelling, punctuation, and form.

◊ Research current day astronomers in the space industry (NASA). What type of education is necessary? What is the advantage/ disadvantage of working with large industry?

◊ Write a story. For example, "It was a beautiful spring day and my family was taking a walk in _____ Park. I was leading the way with my (brother, sister, or friend) and was pretty far ahead when I noticed drops of blood on the path. I called back for my parents and they were nowhere in sight. I decided to..." (Write an open-ended story for someone else to finish. Variation: Do this activity orally with each person adding a paragraph. Continue until the story ends. Tape your story.)

◊ How did Carolus Linnaeus' belief in Biblical Creation lead him to the development of a classification system? (He observed that everything reproduced according to kind and there were no transitions.)

◊ Create a headline and lead story for a secular newspaper with the discovery that the Creation account is true. What caused this discovery? What are secular scientists saying?

◊ Why is Latin a good language for scientific nomenclature (naming)?

◊ Write a short play in which you explore the life and times of Pasteur (or Linnaeus). Include an interview in which you discuss the merits of his contribution to science.

◊ Explain why a "simple cell" such as a gymnosperm spore (plant) is not really simple.

◊ Observe several people for a period of one week. Record facial expression, emotional state, i.e., sad, happy, fearful, suspicious, anxious, etc.

See if you can recognize body language as a means of communication and emotional state.

◊ Stage a "Creation vs. Evolution" debate. Be prepared to explain the problems with the big bang theory and "claims" scientists have made without any proof to back up their claims. (See teaching outline for information.)

◊ Be prepared to debate both sides of this issue: Explain why it would be necessary for primates to evolve speech when they could communicate effectively with gestures. (Evolutionists say we came from primates; Creationists say God created us with the ability to speak and think.)

◊ Play charades depicting various body parts. Have others guess what you are.

◊ Write a comparison between the body, soul, and spirit.

◊ Make up your own language. Be creative.

Math Reinforcement Ideas
9-12

◊   Learn about the metric system. Why is this used in scientific experimentation?

◊   Make a chart of metric equivalents, using linear measurements such as inches, feet, yards, and miles converted to centimeters, meters, and kilometers. Also convert liquid measurements: ounces to grams and quarts to liters and milliliters.

◊   What is the difference between a word equation and a symbol equation? How are these used in scientific experimentation?

◊   How long does it take food to travel through the digestive system? Include the time it takes to chew, swallow, time in the stomach, small inThtestines and large intestines. Why is this knowledge important for medical tests and surgeries?

◊   What is the value of the human body in relation to its elements? What is the value of its molecular compounds? What is the value of human life in relation to the *Bible*? How do these compare? Draw an analogy.

◊   Make a chart of your pulse taken several times a day for a week. Make sure you measure your pulse before getting out of bed, after a meal, and after some sort of exercise. Do this at the same time each day. How do they compare? Variation: extend this activity over a longer period of time. Chart how your physical condition (i.e., sickness) affects your pulse.

◊ Take your body temperature at least three times a day. (Make sure you use the same type of thermometer each time.) Take your temperature before getting out of bed and at different times during the day. Make sure to take your temperature as close as you can to the same times each day. How does illness affect your temperature? Why? (The infection fighting white cells, called lymphocytes, release chemicals which cause inflammation and elevate temperature.)

◊ Give the technical definition of a calorie and explain how different exercises burn calories at different rates. Make a chart of different activities and exercises, and list the amount of calories each burns.

◊ How did Isaac Newton invent calculus? What is calculus used for?

◊ Chart the growth and development of a newborn (if you happen to be blessed with one). Note movements when they first find their hands, feet, other objects, smile, etc. Keep a careful record.

◊ What is the statistical probability of two births producing identical children? (*Adam and Evolution*)

◊ What are the statistics of people recovering from different types of illness? Categorize groups, such as childhood illnesses: asthma, measles, chickenpox, mumps, German measles, colds, tonsillitis; or adult illnesses, such as tuberculosis, meningitis, cancer (various kinds), diabetes, laryngitis, etc. What is the recovery time period? What is the success rate of medication or

◊

treatment? Does belief in God make a difference to the overall well being of a person? List examples of how prayer has healed people. Make a chart of your results.

◊ Study the shapes of the body. What geometric figures can be drawn using straight lines? For example, trace your hand on a sheet of paper. Now, using a ruler and a pencil, follow the pattern of the hand, drawing straight lines. How many sides does your shape have? (6) Does this form have a geometric name? (A 6-sided polygon is a hexagon.)

◊ Study Leonardi da Vinci's drawing of "Vitruvius Man" (There is a picture on page 16 of *How the Body Works* and on the cover of this book!). The hands are extended and so are the legs. What geometric figure is drawn around the figure of the man? What does this tell about the proportions of the human body?

◊ Study body measurements and their uses in historic times. What measurement system can you devise using your body?

◊ How symmetrical is your face? Take a photograph of your face. When developing the film, ask to also have the reversed image developed. Draw a line exactly down the middle of both and cut them in half. Place the left half of the regular image with the right half the reversed image and vice versa. Do the faces look alike? (*How the Body Works*)

◊ How far can you throw different objects? Try a broom stick, football, baseball, rubber ball, etc. Compare several children of different ages and their abilities. Chart your results. Does age play a difference in ability? Why?

◊ Study movement of the body and identify first-order, second-order and third-order levers. In the body the lever is a bone and the effort is the muscle, and the load is the weight of the body which the bone supports. Move different parts of your body and identify which types of levers are involved. Draw a picture or examine your arm from the elbow to the wrist and draw a diagram of the lever underneath it. (*How the Body Works*)

◊ What are the percentages of water loss from the body? List the amounts that are lost from sweat, feces, evaporation, and urine.

◊ Study reflexes. What are the differences in reflexes of a newborn and older children? Devise an experiment to test your reflexes.

Science Activities and Experiments
9-12

Remember to wash your hands and surrounding area thoroughly with anti-bacterial soap after dissecting or handling raw meat! See page introduction for scientific method information and the forms at the end of this manual may be used for experimentation.

◊ Take a glass of water and add several teaspoons of salt to it. What happens? (This is an example of a decomposition reaction. The water molecules break the bonding of the salt crystals into sodium and chlorine ions.) Continue to add salt, a teaspoon at a time, until no more salt will dissolve. Keep track of how many teaspoons you have added. Now heat the solution. Can you add more salt? Record how much salt you added in all. Let the water evaporate and observe. Why did this happen?

◊ Study atomic bonding which forms molecules. For example, ionic bonding in salt: salt is made up of sodium and chlorine (NaCl). A sodium (Na) atom will readily give up an electron, forming a sodium ion with a positive charge. A chlorine atom (Cl) will readily receive an extra electron and form a negatively charged ion. When these two ions combine they form a molecule with an ionic bond. (Find more information in the *Usborne Dictionary of Science*.)

◊ Study covalent bonding. For example, two ions share an electron(s) which orbit both nuclei. (Find more information in the *Usborne Dictionary of Science*.)

◊ Compare carbon atoms in coal and diamonds. Diamonds are much harder because of the crystalline structure of the carbon atoms. This relates to the strength of the bones. The dense crystalline structure of the calcium and phosphorous atoms give bones their strength.

◊ Have your child learn the technical and common names of some of the bones of the skeleton.

◊ Have your child learn which pairs of muscles work in opposition, such as triceps and biceps.

◊ Bones get some strength from their cylindrical shape. Demonstrate this by rolling a few sheets of paper into a tube and balancing a heavy book on it.

◊ Try standing still for a short while. What happens? Why does this happen?

◊ What effect does a high sodium diet or an increase of water have on the amount of times you urinate? Try to vary your diet and find out.

◊ Sprinkle salt on raw meat or celery. What happens? (This is what happens to body cells when the blood fluid is too salty.) Salt absorbs moisture as the meat or celery dries up and cells lose their fluid.

◊ Soak raw meat or celery overnight in warm water. Observe the results. (Water overfills the cells and they burst, the effect can be observed.)

◊ Look up and study DNA though research of the following scientists: Carolus Linnaeus, Gregor Mendel, Francesco Redi, Louis Pasteur.

◊ Write a simple program to draw a box using computer language such as basic. How difficult is this to do?

◊ Write out the chemical name for hemoglobin. What do the letters stand for? (See teaching outline.)

◊ Do animal dissections using resources on page 147. Or dissect raw cuts of meat such as chicken. (*Blood and Guts*)

◊ Use an empty tin can and remove both ends. Stretch a balloon over one end and fasten it with a rubber band. Attach a small mirror on the balloon with glue. Have someone talk into the can and watch the effect of the balloon. (This simulates the larynx.)

◊ Pick up a chair by consciously telling each muscle what to do instead of letting your brain do it automatically.

◊ Plan a menu and analyze the nutritional information. Try to choose a well balanced menu that is low in fat. Take into consideration your family's needs (does anyone need to lose weight? gain weight? have allergies? diabetes? etc.) Variation: Plan a menu for a week or month.

◊ What is spontaneous generation? How did Louis Pasteur's experiment with nutrient (chicken) broth disprove it?

◊ Explain the difference between an atom, an element and a molecule. (*Usborne Dictionary of Science*)

◊ Learn how to use a periodic table with element names, symbol, mass, atomic number, mass number, valence (positive and negative charge), and family groups. (*Usborne Dictionary of Science*)

◊ Study cell structure and name parts.

◊ What is the sugar content of foods? Choose a variety of foods and research the contents. Which foods are highest in sugars?

◊ Take two cubes of sugar and place each one on a separate fireproof plate. Set both on fire, but place a glass over one. What happens? (The sugar is the fuel and oxygen must be present for it to burn.)

◊ The fossil record only shows stasis (species staying the same) or extinction (species going out of existence)of species. How does this contradict the theory of evolution? (Where are the transitional fossils?)

◊ Place a piece of cooked potato on your tongue and do not swallow. How long does it take until the taste changes? Why? (Saliva begins to break down the starch into sugars.)

◊ Using a basic chemistry set (such as the Smithsonian), do experiments dealing with titration. Titration is a process that measures the amount of acids and bases in a solution.

◊ Interview an animal breeder about how desired characteristics are maintained in a breed. Explain in terms of genetics and heredity. Argue pro and con for the physical and moral effects of genetic engineering in humans.

◊ Study the work of Sir Francis Crick, who discovered DNA. Explain how his analysis of DNA changed his ideas about evolution.

◊ Collect a sample of pond water and develop your own system to classify the organisms found. (You will need a microscope for this activity.)

◊ Identify and classify muscles. Variation: identify and classify joints.

◊ Keep track of the number of calories you consume in a day. What is the suggested caloric intake for your age and body type? What can you do to change your diet?

◊ Research sources of various vitamins and minerals. What beneficial effects do you get from these?

◊ Use the exercise chart on page 161. Before beginning, record your weight and body measurements. Over a period of time what effect does exercise have on your body? On your pulse rate?

◊ Analyze dust in your home. Use a microscope or hand lens. What makes up dust? (See the teaching outline.)

◊ Plug your nose while blindfolded and have someone feed you bits of onion, cheese, and apple. Try to discern what item you are eating. Why do you have difficulty?

◊ Contact the *American Cancer Society* or *Lung Association* for resource information and write a paper on the negative effects smoking has on the lungs. (See page 148 for addresses.)

◊ Chart the different areas of your brain that control your actions. How much of the brain do we actually use?

◊ Study the Braille system. How does this relate to the nervous system?

◊ Describe a biosphere. What is it and what is its significance?

◊ Study the science of body movement. What is this called? (kinesiology)

Geography and History Ideas
9-12

◊ Study the history of anatomy. Note the different beliefs through the ages. When did scientists' beliefs begin to change? What was happening in the world? How did the scientific beliefs change the thinking at the time? Compare the Seventeenth through Twentieth centuries.

◊ Compare the early findings about the origins of the universe through the centuries. Use a chart and list the changes in belief as they began to be stated publicly. What was happening in history during this time?

◊ What is a "one world government"? Is this a good thing? When is it a problem? Study what is happening in the European countries in relation to currency. Discuss your opinion.

◊ Research the population explosion myth. Why does this seem to be taken as a fact in the media? What do the World Conferences, such as the (1995) Beijing Conference, have as their agenda? What other World Conferences have taken place recently? What U.S. state could hold all of the population in the world, and how much space would each person have? (The entire population of the world would fit into the state of Texas allowing 1000-1200 square feet for each individual.)

◊ What was the common diet in the Middle Ages as recommended by physicians? (Meat, potato, cheese and bread.) Why? (They thought that those items contained the only nutritional value and vegetables were so fibrous they would have little nutritional value and fruit was so watery it had no nutritional value at all.) How does this compare to the original diet in the Bible? Compare to a healthy diet today.

◊ Use a world map to plot the places where the following scientists are from: Robert Boyle, Michael Faraday, Leonardo da Vinci, Johann Kepler, Joseph Lister, Isaac Newton, Blaise Pascal, Louis Pasteur, William Ramsay, Bernhard Riemann, James Simpson, Nicholas Steno, George Stokes, Rudolph Virchow, John Woodward.

◊ Research and trace the travels of Christ. How large of an area was this?

◊ Research and plot on a map the travels of the Apostle Paul as he spread the Gospel. (He was ministering to the Body of Christ.)

◊ Research the development of government and laws throughout civilization. Variation: study Egyptians, Phoenicians, Romans, etc.

◊ Discuss the impact of the work of missionaries. (Pick a missionary and study the changes that have occurred through his efforts.)

◊ How did the advancement of the Roman Empire prior to the birth of Christ help *pave the way* for the spread of the Gospel? (Infrastructure)

◊ Describe your habitat. Start from small and go to big. Describe in detail your room, house, street, city, state, country, planet, solar system, universe.

◊ Describe different environments. What adaptations are there to various climates? What is macroevolution?

Art and Music Ideas
9-12

Art

◊ Draw a diagram of the vocal cords when someone is talking and when someone is not.

◊ Draw a cell and label its parts.

◊ Use Tinker Toys® to build a molecule of ethylene, methane, propane, or polyethylene.

◊ Study the different styles of painters of the Renaissance, Impressionism, Pointillism, and Abstractism.

◊ Can you draw a portrait that looks like the person you are drawing? Learn to draw portraits. What makes drawing them so difficult?

◊ Make a batik of a body. Decide on a design, perhaps a person watching a sunset at the edge of a lake with mountains in the background. Lightly draw it on a piece of white fabric (old sheets work great). Light a candle and drip hot wax on places where you don't want any color to appear. Make sure the wax forms a thick coating. Mix a dye in a bowl (following instructions on the package) and wearing rubber gloves, dip pieces of your fabric into the dye to stain the material. If you decide to use more than one color, paint on the dye with a brush. Make sure your surface will allow the dye to soak the material (without ruining your furniture!). Use different dyes for the sky, mountains, lake, sunset, body, etc. Rinse the fabric and let it dry. Peel off as much wax as you can, then put it between two pieces of paper bag and iron both sides with a hot iron. The wax will melt and there will be no color where the wax was. You may want to try a really simple drawing at first until you master the technique. (This is a great outdoor activity!)

Music

◊ Study the orchestra. Go to a performance and observe the different sounds each of the instruments makes.

◊ Learn to play an instrument (or a new instrument). Note the way your body performs, for example: blowing, posture, curvature of fingers, etc.

◊ Study the origin and development of various instruments (such as the piano, flute, guitar, etc.).

◊ Make a musical instrument. Be creative; use bottles, flexible tubing, a plastic straw from a large drinking cup, etc.

◊ Study the classic composers. Which one developed great works while deaf? How could this happen?

SECTION 3: ADDITIONAL RESOURCES

Resources, Books and Multi-Media

Additional Resources

Materials List

Microscope Tips, Interlibrary Loan,

Field Trip Guide

Scientific Method Sheets

Activity Sheets

Glossary of Terms

References

Media Angels, Inc.

Resource Books/Multi-Media

Here are some *suggested* resources for doing this unit. Some of these books are Creation Science books and may be purchased from the publishers. Find online.

A Drop of Blood Paul Showers, Harper & Row (K-3)

Bacteria and Viruses: A New True Book Leslie Jean LeMaster, Children's Press, Chicago, 1985 (K-3)

Barron's First Aid for Kids Gary R. Fleisher, M.D., Barron's Educational Series, Inc. 1987 (K-6)

The Body Book Easy to Make Hands-On Models that Teach, Donald M. Silver and Patricia J. Wynne, Scholastic, 1993 (3-8)

Body Talk: The Digestive System, Jenny Bryan, Dillon Press, 1992 (3-8)

Catching a Cold Steve Parker, Franklin Watts, 1991 (K-5)

The Ear and Hearing, Steve Parker, Franklin Watts, 1989 (3-8)

The Edible Pyramid Good Eating Every Day, Loreen Leedy, Holiday House, 1994 (K-3)

Exploring Your Skeleton: Funny Bones and Not-So-Funny Bones, Pamela R. Bishop, Franklin Watts, 1991 (K-3)

Facts and Lists Usborne, EDC Publishing, 1989 (K-12)

Food and Digestion Steve Parker, Franklin Watts, 1990 (3-8)

Germs: Mysterious Microorganisms Encyclopedia of Discovery and Invention, Don Nardo, Lucent Books, Inc. 1991 (3-9)

Hearing, Lillian Wright, Raintree Steck-Vaughn, 1995 (K-3)

Indoor Trips that Teach Magos and Hornnes, The Monkey Sisters, Inc., 1988 (K-6)

Look at Hair Ruth Thomson, Franklin Watts, 1988 (K-3)

The Magic School Bus Inside The Human Body, Joanna Cole, Scholastic Productions, Inc., 1989 (K-3)

The Magic School Bus Inside Ralphie A Book About Germs, John May and Jocelyn Stevenson, Scholastic Productions, Inc., 1995 (K-3)

Men of Science Men of God Morris, Master Books, 1993 (4-12)

The Muscular System, Silverstein, Silverstein, Silverstein, Henry Holt and Co. Inc., 1994. (5-9)

My Feet Aliki, Thomas Y. Crowell, 1990 (K-2)
The Nervous System, Dr. Alvin Silverstein, Virginia Silverstein, & Robert Silverstein, Twenty-First Century Books, 1994 (4-9)

See How I Grow Angela Wilkes, Dorling Kindersley Publishing, 1994 (K-3)

Science Through Art, Andrew Charman, Franklin Watts, 1992 (K-6)

Seeing Lillian Wright, Raintree Steck-Vaughn, 1995 (K-3)

Skin and Its Care Brian Ward, Franklin Watts, 1990 (3-8)

Smelling and Tasting, Lillian Wright, Raintree Steck-Vaughn, 1995 (K-3)

The Story of Your Foot, Dr. Alvin Silverstein and Virginia Silverstein, G.P. Putnam's Sons, 1987 (3-8)

Touching, Lillian Wright, Steck-Vaughn Co., 1995 (K-3)

The Usborne Dictionary of Science Physics, Chemistry and Biology Facts Usborne, EDC Publishing, 1988 (7-12)

Usborne Essential Guides Essential Science, Usborne, EDC Publishing (4-8)

Unlocking the Mysteries of Creation, Dennis Peterson, Creation Resource Foundation, 1986. (K-12)

The Visual Dictionary of the Human Body Eyewitness Dictionaries, Project Editor Mary Lindsay, Dorling Kindersley Books, 1991 (6-12) (Body silhouettes on page 7 may be offensive)

Why Does My Nose Run? And Other Questions Kids Ask About Their Bodies, Joanne Settel and Nancy Baggett, McClelland & Stewart, Ltd, 1985 (K-6)

Why Do Our Bodies Stop Growing, Whitfield & Whitfield, Viking Penguin Inc., 1988 (3-8)

The World of the Microscope Usborne Science and Experiments, EDC Publishing, 1989 (K-8)

Your Brain and Nervous System A New True Book, Leslie LeMaster Regensteiner Publishing Enterprises, Inc. 1984 (K-3)

You Can't Make a Move Without Your Muscles Paul Showers Thomas Y. Crowell, 1982 (K-2)

Your Skin and Mine Paul Showers Thomas Y. Crowell, 1965 (K-3)

Your World: 2000 Health Ron Taylor Facts on File Publications, 1985
(4-8) (Caution: Some pictures may be unsuitable for children. Please preview first.)

Videos: Available in limited quality on Amazon or eBay or search on YouTube

Tell Me Why: A Healthy Body and Medicine Prism Entertainment (K-12) Our family's favorite series of educational videos. Informative, and best of all, the children remember the information! This is a secular video but most children can easily spot evolutionary claims. [Short clip on YouTube]

CD or Mp3—Amazon

Wee Sing Around the World Geography Songs Audio Memory (K-12)
Wee Sing Around the Campfire (K-12)
Wee Sing Bible (K-5)

Activities

Visible Man—available as of this printing on American Science and Surplus: https://www.sciplus.com/

My Body Patricia Carratello, Smith Publications, 1980 (K-5)
Reproducible body organs that can be cut out, colored, and attached to a "life-size" body.

Coloring Books

Human Anatomy Coloring Book, Dover Publications, (7-12) Great drawings of the human body
The Anatomy Coloring Book, Harper Collins, (10-12) High school or older! Very detailed drawings and terminology for upper levels
The Biology Coloring Book, Harper & Row, (9-12) Detailed drawings of DNA, cells, chromosomes and much more. A great alternative for those of us without access to a microbiology lab!
The Human Body Instructional Fair, (3-6) A good coloring book for the younger grades

Games:
SomeBody, The Human Anatomy Game Aristoplay, Ltd. (K-6)
Scientists Card Game, Aristoplay, Ltd. (1-12)
Where in the World?, Aristoplay, Ltd. (8 and up.)

Other Books of Interest that help with unit studies

Elements of Style by Strunk/White (6-12)
        Good grammar **reference** book
English from the Roots Up Volume I Lundquist (4-12)
        Has origins of many common words
If You're Trying to Teach Kids How to Write You've Gotta Have This Book! Marjorie Frank (K-6)
        Great book with lots of good ideas
Music: Invent Your Own Faulhaber, Underhill (K-6)
        A great book teaching music theory in a simple manner
Religious Favorites published by Kjos West (K-12)
        Contains the old-time favorites
Story of Music Usborne (K-12)
        History of music!

Internet:

History World —
        http://www.hyperhistory.com/
is a good site for looking up historical information. Its stated "aim is to make world history more easily accessible through interactive narratives and timelines." I found a fascinating article on origin of Language.

Kids Health, Nemours, nonprofit organizations devoted to children's health.
 http//www.kidshealth.org
 This site has great diagrams and explanations on how the body works. Stick to the kids site as the teen site may have objectionable material.

The Museum of Health & Medicine in Texas
        This told about the museums' features such as the Amazing Body Pavilion including giant human organ models, hands-on exhibits and more. An interesting feature is if you are planning to visit they offer a planning guide ahead of time. I can see how this would save time to preview the exhibits you wanted to see. If you're ever near Hermann Park in Texas, this would be the place to visit. They even have traveling exhibitions.

Research in Human Biology: Kahn Academy — khanacademy.org/science/biology/human-biology
        Videos on different systems of the body with a focus on biology:

The Heart: A Virtual Exploration—http://thevirtualheart.org/
        This contained interactive information about the heart. Here are some Creation science addresses you may want to try:
 The Institute for Creation Research (ICR) Dr. John Morris, President
        http://www.icr.org/creation-science
        Answers in Genesis: Ken Ham
        answersingenesis.org
 The Creation Research Society
        https://www.creationresearch.org

Discovery Channel —preview video to be sure they are age appropriate.
        Discovery.com/tv-shows/other-shows/videos/other-shows-human-body-videos/

Media Angels:
        http:\\www.MediaAngels.com

Additional Resources

Institute for Creation Research	Research information, museum, trips, etc.	ICR.org Discovery center: ICR.org/discoverycenter/
Creation Studies Institute Tom DeRosa	Fossil floats, Museum, educational resources	http:// www.creationstudies.org/
Answers in Genesis Ken Ham	Research, info, trips, Creation Museum	www.answersingenesis.org
Home Training Tools	Resources and supplies from a homeschool owned company	www. hometrainingtools.com
Ring of Fire Science for Kids	Rock sets and geology supplies and curriculum	ring-of-fire.com
Carolina Supply Company	Science focused supply company	www.carolina.com
Nasco Science	Science kits, rocks, minerals, charts, etc.	www.enasco.com
Delta Education	Educational supply company, earth science materials, videos, kits.	delta-education.com
Christian Book Distributors	Christian online book company	christianbook.com
American Science and Surplus	Secular company but has some neat stuff	sciplus.com/

Scientific and Government Resources

Internet sites listed, these may change as we all know. Use caution and your own discretion when visiting any websites.

American Heart Association http://www.heart.org/HEARTORG/	American Lung Association http://www.lung.org/
National Geographic Society http://shop.nationalgeographic.com/	American Cancer Society http://www.cancer.org/
Smithsonian Institute https://www.si.edu/	National Geographic Society Educational http://nationalgeographic.org/education/
National Geographic Society http://www.nationalgeographic.com/	Creation http://www.creation.org/
Human Life International http://www.hli.org/	Institute for Creation Research http://www.icr.org http://www.icr.org/creation-anatomy
Creation Science Ministries http://creationministries.org/	Answers in Genesis https://answersingenesis.org/

Materials List

baggies (clear)	
balance scale (science catalogs)	
balloons	
balls (various sizes)	
Bunsen burner (older grades, order from science catalogs)	
candles	
clay	
containers (various sizes)	
dropper (or use a straw)	
glass beaker (with metric) or glass jar	
measuring cup (metric)	
electric microscope	
paint brush	
paper clips	
plaster of Paris	
poster board	
poster paper	
ruler (with metric)	
scissors	
small stones (or marbles)	
tape	
test tubes (various sizes, order from science catalogs)	
thermometer	
timer	

Microscope Tips

There are many microscopes and the prices range from the inexpensive to the ridiculous (for my budget anyway!). I prefer to use the Blister® Microscope which is no longer made. Searching on eBay or online you may find one—these things were built to last. Look for a compound microscope. These days microscopes are much better than their predecessors. You can use translucent objects, homemade slides or professional slides. Look for microscopes with a 50X lens and 25X and 100X. Unless you have a microbiology or medical student in the making, a basic microscope does a very good job in taking you from K-12 without breaking your budget. Care is minimal. Keep it covered with a lightweight cloth. Wipe it after each use and store it unplugged.

I purchased a very expensive microscope for our homeschool since my children loved science. Unfortunately for me, they continued to use the cheaper microscope for the simple reason that it was easier to use. Word to the wise, buy a cheaper scope!

A Homemade Stain for Slides
Materials:

Red food coloring	Dropper
Blue food coloring	Rubbing alcohol
Small glass jar	Measuring spoons

Directions:

Take a tablespoon and drop two drops of red food coloring and two drops of blue food coloring into the spoon. Fill the remainder of the spoon with rubbing alcohol. Store this in a small jar with a lid. Use this mixture to make slides to view under a microscope. The items on the slide will be easier to view.

Interlibrary Loan

Practically any book you need can be obtained by your *local* library! Yes, even if your town has a limited library or the large downtown library is many miles away. You can do this various ways (check your library to find out the specific procedure).

Our library has a standard procedure. First check the bookshelves, or if you are fortunate this can be done online. The books are listed by (title, author, subject area, etc.) If computers are available the information will include whether or not the book is available at your local branch or at another library. Some cities allow you to reserve books online and walk to the front desk to pick them up! What a time saver especially for those with young children. If the title is not available, you can request it from the librarian. If your library is not computerized, check the card catalog for the book you need and look on the shelf.

If you can't find the book you need, go to the information desk, or in some libraries the check-out counter. Once the book is requested, you will be notified by the library when it comes in. You will have 2 or 3 days to go and pick up your book (or you will lose it). I learned (thanks to a friend, Kristina Krulikas) that the library is not limited to other public libraries. They search private libraries as well for the information you wish! Therefore, some of the harder to obtain books (such as Creation Science) and older books are often available. I know that libraries have ordered Media Angels titles because of repeated requests from patrons. Even our novels have found their way into the public library system due to private schools making them "mandatory" summer reading. (Thank-you, Lord!)

The drawback to ordering books via the library system is that you must be prepared well in advance of doing your study, and the books may not be available when you need them. Searching out your resources should be one of the first things you do in planning your unit study.

Field Trip Guide

Medical Centers
      Dentist
      Optometrist
      Orthopedic Surgeon
      Orthodontist
      Pediatrician
      Hospital
            Pathology Department
            Microbiology Lab
            EKG
            X-ray

Beauty Salon
      Art of hair coloring
      Manicurist

Museum

Labs
      University Laboratory: Observe electron microscope
      Biology Lab

Pharmaceutical House

Creation Science Institute Peace River (Arcadia, Florida) Canoe Trip
      This is a canoe and camping trip and fossil hunt led by Creation Scientists! A great opportunity to learn about science and for great star- gazing! Check the CSI website for information about when their trip will take place. Usually scheduled twice a year in the fall and spring.

Planning a Field Trip

Check Off List	
1. Decide where you wish to visit. Call and check into dates, times and cost.	
2. List contact name, address, phone numbers, directions and travel time.	
3. List your goals and objectives. What do you want the children to learn?	
4. Determine questions you would like your children to answer.	
5. Schedule a time and day to go on the trip: Day:_____ Time:	
6. Check out place ahead of time if possible. Determine if there are any specific rules that need to be followed. List.	
7. Make a list of items to bring.	
8. Go on the field trip.	
9. Find the answers to questions.	
10. Ask field trip guide for suggestions for other trips.	
11. Write a thank-you note. (Great activity for students!)	

SCIENCE EXPERIMENTS

TITLE OF MY EXPERIMENT

_____

Question: (What is the experiment about?)_____

_____

My Guess: (What I think will happen?):_____

_____

Materials: (What I used)_____

_____

What I did:_____

_____

What happened? _____

_____

_____

Why did it happen?_____

_____

SCIENCE EXPERIMENTS

Question: (What is the experiment about?)

My Guess: (What I think will happen?):

Materials:

What did I do?

What Happened? BEFORE PICTURE	What Happened? AFTER PICTURE

Why did it happen?

SCIENCE EXPERIMENTS

Question:_____
_____
_____

Hypothesis:_____
_____
_____
_____

Materials:_____
_____
_____
_____

Procedure:_____
_____
_____
_____
_____
_____

Observation/Data:_____
_____
_____
_____
_____

Conclusion:_____
_____
_____
_____
_____
_____
_____

Pulse Rates

Name:_____

Take your pulse rates during different times of the day. Measure your pulse for 30 seconds and multiply by two to get your pulse rate for one minute. Record the amounts for one week. Do this with other people in the family. Try to do this at the same time each day.

	Pulse Rate Waking Up Time:	Pulse Rate After Breakfast Time:	Pulse Rate Before Lunch Time:	Pulse Rate Before Dinner Time:	Pulse Rate Before Bed Time:
Monday					
Tuesday					
Wednesday					
Thursday					
Friday					
Saturday					

Pulse Rates and exercise

Name:_____

Take your pulse rates at rest and after doing exercises of your choice. Measure your pulse for 30 seconds and multiply by two to get your pulse rate for one minute. Record the amounts for one week. Do this with other people in the family. Try to do this for several weeks. Does your pulse go down as you get used to exercising?

Type of Exercise and Number Done:	Pulse Rate at Rest and After doing: Exercise:	Pulse Rate at Rest and After doing: Exercise:	Pulse Rate at Rest and After doing: Exercise:	Pulse Rate at Rest and After doing: Exercise:	Pulse Rate at Rest and After doing: Exercise:
Monday					
Tuesday					
Wednesday					
Thursday					
Friday					
Saturday					

Exercise Chart

Directions: Keep track of the following information daily. Measure your body dimensions once a week. Do this for several weeks and compare the information. What did you find? Evaluate your overall physical condition.

Type of Exercise	Duration or Repetition					Pulse Rate				
	M	T	W	TH	F	M	T	W	TH	F
Stretches										
Jumping Jacks										
Sit-Ups or Variations of Sit-Ups										
Toe Touches										
Push-Ups										
Leg Lifts										
Jump Rope										
Jogging										
Weight:										

Body Measurements:

Waist	
Upper Arms	
Upper Thighs	
Hips	
Calves	
Shoulders	
Chest	

Weight Loss Chart

Directions: If someone in your family needs to lose weight this chart will help keep track of your progress! Use this with an exercise program.

Pounds Lost		1	2	3	4	5	6	7	8
	16								
	14								
	12								
	10								
	8								
	6								
	4								
	2								

Weeks

GLOSSARY OF TERMS

alveoli - tiny air sacs at the end of the bronchioles where oxygen passes into the red blood cells

amylase - a digestive enzyme contained in saliva that begins to break down complex starch molecules into simple sugars such as glucose and maltose

antibodies - made by the lymphocytes that recognize and remember certain pathogens that have previously invaded the body

antigens - chemical patterns on germs that stimulates the human body to produce antibodies; these antibodies are produced by the lymphocytes

axon - transmitter that carries nerve impulses to the end of other nerves

basophils - a type of granulocyte that fights infection by releasing chemicals that cause fever and inflammation

brain stem - connects brain and spinal cord; includes thalamus and hypothalamus which control sleep, hunger, thirst, etc., and the medulla which controls heart rate, breathing, blood pressure and other vital functions

bronchi - tubes that branch from the windpipe (trachea), one for each lung

bronchioles - branches from the bronchi that become smaller and smaller

cecum - a pouch at the beginning of the large intestine that receives matter from the small intestines

cerebral cortex - surface of the cerebrum where most of the brain's information is stored

cerebellum - means 'little cerebrum' and is 1/8 the size of the cerebrum; controls equilibrium and muscle movement

cerebrum - the two major halves or hemispheres of the brain, divided into lobes, said to be the location of intelligence and learning

circadian rhythms - A daily rhythmic cycle, based on 24-hour intervals

cochlea - the spiral-shaped portion of the inner ear that contains the perilymph fluid that conducts vibrations

colon - consists of the ascending, transverse, and descending portions; the first half of the colon absorbs water and the second half stores the feces

condyle - the oval shaped head (the rounded process at the end of a bone) of bone that articulates in the cavity (hollow part) of another bone

corpus callosum - that part of the brain that links both hemispheres so that they work in unison

cytoplasm - the gel substance on the inside of the cell which contains all other cell structures

deoxyribonucleic acid - known as DNA, is a molecule that contains two chains, of thousands of nucleotides, made from the sugar deoxyribose (deoxyribose sugar has one less oxygen atom that the ribose sugar), that wind around each other to form a helix; DNA is found in the nucleus of the cell and contains all of the body's hereditary information

dermis - layer of skin beneath the outer layer, that gives the skin its nutrition; contains hair follicles, nerves, sweat glands, and sensory receptors

diffusion - The spontaneous mixing of the particles of two or more substances as a result of random motion.

duodenum - the first part of the small intestine that receives the processed food from the stomach that is now in the form of a paste

end enzymes - digestive enzymes that each match only one certain nutrient, when one meets a matching enzymes, the nutrient is quickly absorbed

epidermis - the outer most layer of the skin , also called the horny layer, that contains skin cells in the last stages before flaking off; the basal layer of the epidermis contains live cells

epiglottis - a flap of tissue that closes automatically over the top of the windpipe to prevent food from entering the trachea and the lungs

epithelial cells - cover the surface of the villi that line the small intestine; these cells absorb nutrients

erthrocytes - human red blood corpuscles, found in the bone marrow of long bones

extensors - muscles that are used to straighten, or extend, a joint

fibrinogen - a globulin substance in the blood that is converted to fibrin by the platelets forming a mesh of fibers, which along with the platelets form a clot

flexors - muscles that are used to bend or flex a joint

ganglia (ganglion) - point where a number of nerve cells come together to form a bundle

glucose - form of sugar in the blood that is used by the body to produce energy

golgi complex - where proteins that are made within the cell are stored until needed

granulocytes - a type of white cell that turns into 1) neutrophils that are the first to attack infection, 2)basophils that release chemicals that cause inflammation, 3) eosinophils that also attack germs

hair cells - attached to a membrane that is moved by the perilymph fluid when sound wave energy passes to the inner ear; smaller hairs attached to the hair cells convert this energy to electrical energy that is sent to the brain; each ear has 16,000 hair cells

hemoglobin - largest molecule in nature that picks up oxygen in the lungs and releases it to the tissues by the process of the iron atoms rusting with the oxygen in order to carry it to the tissue and then unrusting to release the oxygen to the tissue

hypothalamus - a gland that controls pituitary function, communicates with the brain about the sensations of hunger, thirst, temperature, etc.

leucocytes (leukocytes) - general term for white blood corpuscles (actually, they are colorless) that fight infection in the body; larger than red blood cells

lymphocytes - a type of white cell that is produced by the lymph system; fights infection; also able to recognize germs that have previously invaded the body and make antibodies that attack those germs

medulla - part of the brain stem that controls heart rate, breathing, blood pressure and other vital functions

metabolism - the process where oxygen is used to burn glucose in the cells to produce energy for the body

monocytes - a type of white cell that turn into macrophages that eat and digest invading viruses and bacteria (known as pathogens)

myocardium - The muscular wall of the heart, heart muscle

nephrons - structures in the kidneys that cleanse the blood by filtering out waste products

nerve - Bundles of fibers made up of neurons that are conduits for sensory stimuli and motor impulses pass between the brain or other parts of the central nervous system and the body. Nerves form a network of pathways for sending and re ceiveing information throughout the body.

neurons - nerve cells; the basic functioning unit of the nervous system

neurotransmitters - the molecule of acetylcholine which excites the receptors on the membrane of receiving cells and propagate an impulse to the next neuron

nucleotides - building blocks of nucleic acid chains, made of proteins and sugars

olfactory neurons - receptor cells in the nose that combine with mucous to conduct impulses to the brain; odor molecules dissolve in the mucus and stimu- late the sense of smell

osteoblasts - cells where new bone tissue is formed

osteoclasts - cells that dissolve and reabsorb bone tissue

parathyroid - located behind the thyroid, regulate the amount of calcium in the blood

parotid glands - one of three pairs of salivary glands that produce about 1.5 quarts of fluid every day; these are the glands that become swollen when you have the mumps

pericardium - a cone shaped, membranous sac that contains the heart

perilymph fluid - fluid contained in the cochlea; motion of this fluid is transferred to the hair cells and then to electrical impulses to the brain for hearing

perisoteum - a thin layer of material covering bones that contains the nerves and vessels that feed the bones

phagocytosis - process by which invading germs are destroyed; monocytes, eosinophils and neutrophils actually eat and digest bacteria and viruses

pineal gland - A small, cone-shaped organ in the brain that secretes the hormone melatonin. Scientists are not certain what function the pineal has.

platelets - much smaller than red blood cells; important in repairing injuries to tissue

pleura - a moist membrane that covers the lungs and the inside of the chest cavity to allow the lungs to move easily when inhaling and exhaling

porphyrin - part of the hemoglobin molecule that carries oxygen; can only exist in an oxygen-rich environment and would be chemically destructive to amino acids

rectum - the end of the large intestine through which feces is moved to the anus to be eliminated

ribonucleic acid - known as RNA; strands of nucleotides made from the sugar ri- bose, that join together to form the type of nucleic acid - ribonucleic acid

serous fluid - produced by the serous glands at the back of the tongue; contains the chemicals that begin the digestion process by breaking down starches into sugars

somatosensory cortex - processes information from the senses and all parts of the body

stereo cilia - very tiny hairs on top of the hair cells within the cochlea that brush up against a membrane that send electrical impulses to the brain

substrate - the material or substance upon which an enzyme acts; the surface on which a plant or animal grows or is attached.

synapse - the gap at the junction of two neurons across which information, in the form of a nerve impulse, must pass

thalamus - part of the limbic system, located within the cerebrum, relays information from the senses to the cortex

thrombocytes - another name for platelets; they form a clot or thrombus

thrombus - formed when platelets and fibrin come to the site of damaged tissue and repair the damage; also know as a clot

thymus - controls production of white cells in children, no known function in adults

tympanic membrane - the eardrum; a membrane that divides the outer and middle ear; the hearing process begins when sound energy (vibrations) cause the eardrum to vibrate

villi (villus) - thousands of finger-like protrusions that make up the lining of the small intestine that have the task of absorbing nutrients

References

A.D.A.M.: The Inside Story 1996. Atlanta, GA: A.D.A.M. Software, Inc.

Anatomy Series, Classic Studies in Science for the Young Mind: The Hand. 1992. Lemon Grove, CA: Provision Media

Animal Intelligence. 1995. The Discovery Channel.

Ancient Man. 1995. The Learning Channel. Broadcasting Co.

Baker, Silvia, M.Sc., 1976. *Bone of Contention.* Phillipsburg, New Jersey: Evangelical Press.

Batten, Don. 1997. "Human/ Chimp DNA Similarities." *Creation ex nihilo.* Vol. 19, no. 1, p. 21-22.

Batten, Don. 1997. "Not Another Ape-Man." *Creation ex nihilo.* Vol. 18, no 3, p. 42-45.

Behe, Michael. 1996. *Darwin's Black Box.* New York, New York.: Simon & Schuster: The Free Press.

Bender, Lionel. 1989. *The Body.* New York, N.Y.: Gloucester Press.

Bliss, Richard. 1988. *Origins - Creation or Evolution.* El Cajon, California: Master Books.

Body Atlas. 1995. The Learning Channel. Broadcasting Co.

Body Works. 1995. The Learning Channel. Broadcasting Co.

Broekel, Ray. 1984. *Your Five Senses.* Chicago, IL.: Children's Press.

Brunn, Ruth D., and Bertel Brunn. 1982. *The Human Body.* New York, N.Y.: Random House.

Bryan, Jenny. 1992. *Breathing.* New York ,N.Y.: Dillon Press.

Bryan, Jenny. 1992. *Digestion.* New York, N.Y. :Dillon Press.

Bryan, Jenny. 1992. *Movement.* New York ,N.Y. :Dillon Press.

Caselli, Giovanni. 1978. *The Human Body.* New York, N.Y.: Grosset and Dunlap.

Daniels, Patricia, ed., 1992. *Understanding Science and Nature: Human Body.* Alexandria, VA: Time-Life, Inc.

Doolan, Robert. 1996. "Piltdown Prankster Finally Fingered." *Creation ex nihilo.* Vol. 18, no. 4, p. 39.

Dust or Destiny. Moody Science Classics. video. Chicago, IL: Moody Bible Institute.

Engel, Arieli, Susan L. M.D. 1994. *How Your Body Works.* Emeryville, CA.: Ziff-Davis Press.

Emerson, Paul. 1996. "Eating Out in Eden." *Creation ex nihilo.* Vol. 18, no. 2, pp. 10-13.

Flanagan, Geraldine, L., 1994. *The First Nine Months of Life.* New York, N.Y., Ballantine Books.

Graham, Jean Ann, and Wallace, Louise. 1990. *The Complete Mind & Body Book* N.Y., N.Y.: Simon and Schuster.

Gray, Henry, 1977. *Gray's Anatomy* . New York, NY, Gramercy Books.

Guiness, Alma, E., 1987. *Reader's Digest ABC's of the Human Body.* Pleasantville, NY:Reader's Digest.

James, Peter ,and Nick Thorpe. 1994. *Ancient Inventions.* New York, N.Y.: Ballentine Books.

Hobson, J. Allan. 1989. *Sleep.* N.Y., N.Y: Science American Library.

Human Life International. organization. Front Royal, VA.

Kalmann, Bobby. 1983. *Early Health and Medicine.* New York, N.Y.: Crabtree Publication Co.

Keveren, Phillip. 1992. *The New Illustrated Family Hymn Book.* Milwaukee, WI: Leonard Publishing.

LeVay, David. 1993. *Human Anatomy and Physiology* . Chicago, Illinois: N.T.C. Publishing Group.

Markle, Sandra. 1991. *Outside and Inside You.* New York, N.Y.: Bradbury Press.

Martin, Paul D. 1984. *Messengers to the Brain.* New York, N.Y.: National Geographic Society Books.

McGuire, Jack. 1990. *Care and Feeding of the Brain.* N.Y., N.Y.: Doubleday.

McMurtry, Grady. Speaker. 1994. *Creation Science Seminar.* Bonita Springs, FL.

Morris, Henry M. 1974. *Many Infallible Proofs, Evidences for the Christian Faith.* El Cajon, CA.: Master Books.

"The Mystery of Senses" June 1993, Vol. 14, no. 6, Discover Magazine.

Nine Month Miracle. 1995. Atlanta, GA.: A.D.A.M. Software, Inc.

Parker, Steve. 1989. *The Heart & Blood.* New York, N.Y.: Franklin Watts.

Parker, Steve. 1989. *The Lungs & Breathing.* New York, N.Y.: Franklin Watts.

Petersen, Dennis. 1986. *Unlocking the Mysteries of Creation.* El Dorado, CA: Creation Resource Foundation

Pitman, Michael. 1984. *Adam and Evolution, A Scientific Critique of Neo-Darwinism.*Grand Rapids,MI: Baker Books.

Red River of Life. Moody Science Classics. video. Moody Bible Institute. Chicago, IL.

Restar, Richard, M.D. 1991. *The Brain Has A Mind of It's Own.* New York, N.Y: Harmony Books.

Richards, Lawrence O., 1987. *It Couldn't Just Happen.* Dallas, Texas: Word Publishing.

Rowan, Dr. Pete. 1995. *Some Body.* N.Y., N.Y.: Alfred A. Knoph.

Sanderman, Anna. 1995. *Breathing.* Brookfield, Connecticut: Copper Beech Books.

Seuling, Barbara. 1986. *You Can't Sneeze with Your Eyes Open & Other Freaky Facts About the*

Human Body. New York, N.Y.: Lodestar Books.

Silverstein, Alvin, Virginia Silverstein, and Robert Silverstein. 1970. *Circulatory System: The Rivers Within.* Englewood Cliffs, N.J.: Prentice-Hall, Inc.

Silverstein, Alvin, Virginia Silverstein, and Robert Silverstein. 1994. *Excretory System.* New York, N.Y: Twenty-First Century Books.

Silverstein, Alvin, Virginia Silverstein, and Robert Silverstein. 1994. *Muscular System.* New York, N.Y: Twenty-First Century Books.

Silverstein, Alvin, Virginia Silverstein, and Robert Silverstein. 1994. *Reproductive System.* New York, N.Y: Twenty-First Century Books.

Silverstein, Alvin, Virginia Silverstein, and Robert Silverstein. 1994. *Respiratory System.* New York, N.Y.: Twenty-First Century Books.

Secret of Life at 118 Green Street, The. 1995. The Learning Channel.

Seven Wonders of the World, The. 1995. The Learning Channel. Broadcasting Co.

Smith, Jillyn. 1989. *Senses & Sensibilities.* New York, NY: John Wiley & Sons, Inc.

Stanton, Mary, and Albert Hyma. 1992. *Streams of Civilization Vol. 1.* Arlington Heights, IL.:Christian Lib erty Press.

Steven, Parker. 1994. *The Respiratory System.* New York, NY: Franklin Watts.

Storrs, Graham. 1974. *Understanding the Senses.* Morristown, N.J.: Silver Burdett Co.

Takahata, N. 1995. *A Genetic Perspective on the Origin and History of Humans in the Annual Review of Ecology and Systematics.*

Tapley, Donald, MD. 1989. *Complete Home Medical Guide.* N.Y., N.Y.: Crown Publishers, Inc.

Thompson, Ruth. 1988. *Look at Hair.* N.Y., N.Y.: Franklin Watts.

Ultra Science. 1995. The Learning Channel.

Vannini, Vanio, and Guiliano Pogliani. 1980. *The Color Atlas of the Human Body .* New York, N.Y.: Harmony Books.

Ward, Brian. 1990. *Skin.* New York, N.Y.: Franklin Watts.

Wieland, Carl, ed. 1994. "Armoured Neanderthal." *Creation ex nihilo.* Vol. 16, no. 2, p. 15.

Wieland, Carl, ed. 1994. "Creationist Prediction Confirmed." *Creation ex nihilo.* Vol. 16, no 9, p. 9.

Wieland, Carl, ed. 1994. "Lucy's Knee Problem." *Creation ex nihilo.* Vol. 16, no. 2, p. 31.

Wieland, Carl, ed. 1992. "Shaking Hands with Creation." *Creation ex nihilo.* Vol. 14, no.3, p. 43.

Wieland, Carl, ed. 1995. "The Marvelous Message Molecule." *Creation ex nihilo.* Vol. 17, 4, pp. 10-13.

Wieland, Carl, ed. 1994. "Your Amazing Eyes." *Creation ex nihilo.* Vol. 16, no. 2, pp. 8-9.

Wolf, Burt. 1995. *A Taste for Travel.* Discovery Channel.

Wright, Lillian. 1995. *Smelling and Tasting.* Austin, TX.: Steck-Vaughn Co.

Wright, Lillian. 1995. *Touching.* Austin, TX.: Steck-Vaughn Co.

Xenakis, Alan P. M.D. 1993. *Why Doesn't My Funny Bone Make Me Laugh.* New York, N.Y.: Villard Books.

Yount, Lisa. 1994. *William Harvey; Discoverer of How Blood Circulates.* Hillside, N.J.: Enslow Publishers, Inc.

Yaroch, Lucia Allen. 1996. *Shape Analysis Using the Thin-Plate Spline: Neanderethal Cranial Shape as an Example, written in the Yearbook of Physical Anthropology.*

Creation Science Study Guides **by Felice Gerwitz and Jill Whitlock** $18.95 each
Each fantastic study guide is written from a Biblical Creationist perspective, on three levels spanning K-12. Includes a teaching outline, activities, experiments, activities, resources, reproducible sheets, and much more. These resources will help you with all the planning you need to teach the wonders of God's Creation!
Creation Science: A Study Guide to Creation!
Creation Anatomy: A Study Guide to the Miracles of the Body!
Creation Astronomy: A Study Guide to the Constellations!

Science Hands-On Experiment and Activity Pack by Felice Gerwitz, $12.95 each
These packs contain ready-to-copy activities and experiments, directions, scientific method sheets, games and crossword puzzles, glossary, and much more. This resource complements the unit study guides. *Choose Geology & Creation Science, Anatomy, or Astronomy.*

Creation Classes by Felice Gerwitz, MediaAngels.com—Finally, classes for your children taught by Felice, the best of both worlds. Download on your computer, follow along with the handouts and use the amazing handouts and additional activities. All classes include the hands-on experiment and activity pack. Buy once and use for all your students.

Teaching Science and Having Fun! by Felice Gerwitz, $16.95
This handy teacher's reference includes how to schedule, what to teach, a scope and sequence, the scientific method, how to set up a lab, how to choose a microscope, resources, and much more. Felice, a former classroom teacher, has homeschooled since 1986, holds science workshops for children, and conducts seminars for adults.

An Insider's Guide to Successful Science Fair Projects by Felice Gerwitz, $8.99
A handy guide for helping parents and children put together a winning Science Fair Project! Great science fair strategies, how to plan, where to look for information, the scientific method, keeping a journal, writing a report and abstract, display guidelines, what judges look for, and much more.

Truth Seekers Mystery Series™ by Felice Gerwitz and Christina Gerwitz, $8.99 each.
Creation-based adventure novels for the entire family. You've studied the topic of Creation, now read the books! These faith-filled teen mystery stories will delve into the basic arguments evolutionists use in "proving" their position. Teaches students how to answer these questions in a fun to read, adventure story. You will want to collect the series. Join homeschooled teens Christian and Anna Murphy and their family as they face action, adventure, mystery, and heart-stopping suspense and learn that the truth will set you free! Current titles: *The Missing Link: Found, Dinosaur Quest at Diamond Peak,* and *Keys to the Past: Unlocked.*

Truth Seekers Mystery Series™ Literature Study Guides by Felice Gerwitz $6.50 each
These easy-to-use literature study guides bring the science-based novels to life. Help budding writers in your home study literary techniques in a non-threatening manner. Check for reading and vocabulary comprehension and then study the additional science topics explored in the novels. Easy to use and fun to study! Available for each of the novels above.

<u>Visit MediaAngels.com</u> for additional classes and books.
American History and American Government & Elections Video Classes
Information In A Nutshell: **Writing and Publishing and Business Tips and Taxes For Writers**
Reach for the Stars: **A Young Fiction Author's Workbook**
Fast Track: MicroBusiness For Kids—online interactive website
Homeschooling with Proverbs—Bible study for the entire family

Acknowledgments

Felice would like to thank Steve Shelfer whose remark
about DNA sparked the idea for this unit study!

About the Authors

Felice is happily married and has been a home schooling mother since 1986. She has four homeschool graduates and continues to school her youngest who graduates in 2018. Felice has a degree in Elementary Education, Learning Disabilities, and Early Childhood Education. Felice is an author of science curriculum, has held science workshops for children ages Pre-K to 12, and seminars for parents covering many topics. Felice is the founder and owner of Media Angels, Inc. as well as the UltimateHomeschoolRadioNetwork.com. She podcasts at Vintage-HomeschoolMoms.com, continuing to help and mentor homeschool moms.

Check the Media Angels website for current information about the latest titles at www.MediaAngels.com or e-mail Felice at Felice@MediaAngel.com www.UltimateHomeschoolRadioNetwork.com for homeschool podcasts

After graduating from Texas A & M University, Jill worked as an exploration Geologist in Denver Co. In December 1983, she accepted Jesus Christ as her Savior and began praying and studying about the Creation vs. evolution question. The Lord was faithful and brought many people into her path who started her on the way to becoming a Flood Geologist and a young earth Creationist. She now holds Creation Science seminars for churches and other groups. She has been homeschooling since 1986 and has two homeschool graduates and one son she continues to school. Jill died in 2007 and she has been missed. Her work however lives on and it continues to be a blessing.

www.ingramcontent.com/pod-product-compliance
Lightning Source LLC
Chambersburg PA
CBHW080528090426
42733CB00015B/2516